New York
Sweets

New York
Sweets

A SUGARHOUND'S GUIDE TO THE
BEST BAKERIES, ICE CREAM PARLORS,
CANDY SHOPS, AND OTHER
EMPORIA OF DELICIOUS DELIGHTS

Text and photographs by
SUSAN PEAR MEISEL

RIZZOLI
NEW YORK

New York · Paris · London · Milan

**I dedicate this book to my family, my friend
Elisabeth, and my grandson Benjamin.**

Acknowledgments

I would like to begin by thanking Charles Miers for once again giving me the opportunity to have a book published by Rizzoli. Many thanks also to Christopher Steighner for having the faith in me to go it alone—I couldn't have had a better editor. I appreciate the work of LeAnna Weller Smith who created the beautiful design of the book. And, of course I am grateful to all the owners, chefs, and staff of the great establishments included here. The list of shops wouldn't have been what it is without the unending additions from my friend Ann Fredlin, one of the best foodies I know. My friend Shawn Peterson helped me every step of the way. Christian Diaz, a Photoshop genius, made my images look the best they could. Elizabeth Harris was there to save the day every time the computer failed me. Beth Green worked wonders with the Sweets Sampler features. And last but not least, my friend Jane Bishop, with her undying English humor and brilliant writing ability, helped me make my deadlines. I thank all of you for helping to make *New York Sweets* as sweet as it is.

—Susan Pear Meisel

FIRST PUBLISHED IN THE UNITED STATES OF AMERICA IN 2013
BY RIZZOLI INTERNATIONAL PUBLICATIONS, INC.
300 PARK AVENUE SOUTH
NEW YORK, NY 10010
WWW.RIZZOLIUSA.COM

©2013 SUSAN PEAR MEISEL

2013 2014 2015 2016 / 10 9 8 7 6 5 4 3 2 1

PRINTED IN CHINA

DESIGNED BY LEANNA WELLER SMITH

ISBN: 978-0-8478-3961-2

LIBRARY OF CONGRESS CONTROL NUMBER: 2012950105

Contents

INTRODUCTION

I HAVE HAD A LIFELONG LOVE AFFAIR WITH NEW YORK SWEETS. It began when I was a child in my grandmother's kitchen. My grandma owned a shoe store and lived in an apartment just above the store. We would first walk through the shop, then through the back, up a few stairs, and into her kitchen. In the center of the room was a table covered in shiny oilcloth printed with large flowers, and on the center of the table were always a big sugar bowl, a bottle of maple syrup, and a canister that held sweet butter. Grandma's specialty was blintzes. She would cover her kitchen table with dish towels and flip the thin pancakes on them to cool. I was fascinated by the process, and she loved having an audience. When the pancakes had cooled, she would have any of a number of fillings on hand: cherries, apples, blueberries, or a sweet ricotta—cream cheese mixture. After filling them, she'd roll and fold them into lovely sweet presents. These blintzes were delectable. She also made wonderful puddings. My favorites were her warm rice pudding topped with raisins and cinnamon, vanilla custard with crushed vanilla wafers, and chocolate pudding with a dollop of whipped cream. But the pièce de résistance was her apple brown betty. She would bring to the table a steaming hot baking dish filled to the brim with warm apples, butter, brown sugar, and cinnamon, topped with corn flakes and more butter and honey. The aroma was amazing—the taste even better, especially with the scoop of vanilla ice cream melting over the top. My grandmother could satisfy anyone's sweet tooth.

When I was in elementary school, my best friends and I would look forward to an ice cream treat a couple times a week: We'd wait for the three-o'clock bell to ring and then we'd run to line up for the Good Humor man. My favorite was a Creamsicle-type concoction—vanilla ice cream on a stick with an orange ice exterior, and my friends got ice cream sandwiches and ice cream pops. We were happy. But soon the "automatic" ice cream cone came along—a frozen concoction with chocolate sauce and nuts that was wrapped in a spiral of paper that you unraveled, and this quickly became my favorite. I also used to meet my friends after school at the corner store for a chocolate egg cream and a two-cent pretzel—there was some attraction of that mix of salt and chocolate that sticks with me even today.

When school let out for the season, my family and I would spend the summer months in Long Beach, Long Island. As the name suggests, it was very close to the ocean, the beach, and the boardwalk. There were sweet treats galore, from airy cotton candy that was fun to pull apart and eat

APPLE
CIDER
flower
$4.—

before the wind blew it on your face, to soft ice cream that melted down your hand if not licked fast enough and sticky caramel corn that stuck to your teeth. I loved the saltwater taffy in a dozen or so flavors (my favorites were cherry, banana, and chocolate). We enjoyed apples on a stick dipped in bright red sugar candy or caramel. But Dugan's was everyone's favorite. This was a truck that would roll around the neighborhood selling pastries, doughnuts, layer cakes, coffee cakes, and, my very favorite, the box of six cupcakes with strawberry, vanilla, and chocolate icing. My friends and I would carefully transport the box as if it held precious jewels. Then, one by one, we would take the icing, roll it up like a stick of candy, and devour it in seconds. None of us really cared about the cake, but the icing was supreme. Luckily we each liked different flavors so no fighting wrecked the moment.

I had many memorable dessert experiences at restaurants and bakeries around the city. The Horn & Hardart Automat was a place that I still wish existed. The first thing you did when you walked in was change your dollar into a handful of nickels. Then you set your sights on the wall lined with glass-fronted dispensers with every kind of food—pies, cakes, sandwiches, and other savory dishes. I always ran to the desserts. I put my coins in the slot and a door opened to reveal a warm vanilla custard with a hard caramel topping. Although there were many other wonderful choices, including banana cream pie, and apple, blueberry, and cherry pies, I never strayed from my vanilla custard with the brittle sugar top that cracked with a spoon. Going to Horn & Hardart was a cherished Friday-night ritual with my family.

We moved from upper Manhattan to Forest Hills, Queens, when I was in first grade, and that was when I started to take ballet. My friends and I would meet at the Jay Dee Bakery on Queens Boulevard after class, and the vision of Charlotte russes danced in our heads. This individual version consisted of a thin piece of soft lemony sponge cake piled high with homemade whipped cream and topped off with a cherry; it was packaged in little white cardboard cup with a push-up bottom. I remember laughing while we covered our faces in that magic whipped delight. We all saved the cherry for last.

On Sunday mornings it was my responsibility to get the newspaper and the baked goods for breakfast. My parents left money on the kitchen table and all I had to do was walk to the corner to Dave's Bakery. The smell of cinnamon and butter filled the air. There was always a line out the door but still plenty to choose from when I got to the counter. The cinnamon buns and coffee crumb cake were so incredible the memory still lingers with me today. During the walk up the block I would eat the biggest chunks of the crumb-cake topping; by the time I got home there was always a bun missing as well.

Another favorite bakery was Ebinger's, a chain that originated in Brooklyn and expanded into Queens. The dark chocolate blackout cake was filled and frosted with chocolate pudding; chocolate cake crumbs were spread on top. It was the talk of my neighborhood. Ebinger's had a repertoire of about a dozen items in addition to the beloved blackout cake. These included the Othello, a cone-

shaped vanilla cake filled with buttercream and coated in chocolate; a fluffy yellow cake layered with a milk chocolate buttercream and a thousand toasted almonds sprinkled all over; éclairs the size of footballs; and the tart lemon bar with its thin sugar icing that prevented your cheeks from puckering permanently. Sadly, Ebinger's closed but the memory of these sweet treats stays with me to this day.

Desserts have come a long way since I was a child. The simple things I remember eating were the groundwork for the sweets available today. Now, pies are made in every flavor imaginable, such as Salted Caramel Apple from Four & Twenty Blackbirds (page 168) or Crack Pie from Momofuku (page 88). There are ice creams and sorbets in flavors as exotic as bacon and avocado. There are donuts shaped like squares, cupcakes that are works of art, and cakes that come in every flavor, shape, and size. One of the most popular today is the red velvet cake, which has had a resurgence in popularity in recent years, along with its cupcake spin-off.

New York Sweets celebrates desserts and the places where you can buy the best, most inventive, and delicious treats. Over the last few years, there has been an explosion of creative new sweets in the city, and this is one of the reasons I set out to do this book: to cover this exciting renaissance in the world of sugar. My criteria for selecting these purveyors, confectioners, bakers, and artisans were not scientific. But, the most important factor was the quality of ingredients. I wanted to focus on places that used natural and locally sourced components. Also key: each place had to be doing something in a way that set the shop apart. There had to be an individual spirit present in their creations. My love of sweet treats has intensified because of this book—and I know yours will too!

SUSAN PEAR MEISEL

Sweets Sampler: Doughnuts

THE PERFECT DONUT IS AN AIRY CONFECTION THAT ISN'T TOO GREASY OR HEAVY. At best, fresh and sweet, tender yet chewy, they taste as good as they look. They are a simple indulgence adored by children and grownups alike.

DULCE DE LECHE WITH ALMONDS

DOUGH // PG 166

This doughnut is big, hearty, and dense. It's crunchy on the outside but light as air within, with a dulce de leche glaze on top and a sprinkling of toasted almonds.

CRANBERRY DOUGHNUT

DOUGHNUT PLANT // PG 73

This is a chewy yeast doughnut. The proportion of glaze to doughnut is perfect, and there's a lovely super-tart flavor from fresh cranberries.

RASPBERRY JELLY DOUGHNUT

GLASER'S BAKE SHOP // PG 121

An old-school jelly doughnut, it's dusted with sugar and bursting with fruity flavor. And it's just greasy enough to taste terrific.

HONEY-DIPPED DONUT

PETER PAN DONUT & PASTRY SHOP // PG 184

The honey-dipped is your classic glazed doughnut: light and airy. It's an old-fashioned doughnut, perfectly executed.

COFFEE CRUNCH DONUT

BABYCAKES // PG 57

A cake-like doughnut, this is a very tasty, gluten-free treat. Baked, not fried, it is terrifically moist, with a coffee glaze and mini coffee chips and a sugar crumble sprinkled on top.

DONUT SQUARE

CATHCART AND REDDY // PG 62

A new, over-the-top take on the filled doughnut, this is made of a light brioche dough, shaped in a square, and filled with Nutella.

New York Sweets

GREENWICH VILLAGE
AND SOHO

FAVORITE FLAVORS
Stracciatella, Arancia Rossa

Amorino

GELATO AL NATURALE

AMORINO GELATO

A BLOOM OF ICE CREAM

Amorino Gelato is one of those special places that we are lucky to have in New York City. Cristiano and Paolo, childhood friends in Italy, started Amorino in 2002, and it has been a worldwide success ever since. It's located on one of the best corners of Greenwich Village, and the line starts as soon as the doors open in the morning. But the real action is in the evening, when people who are eating dinner or just strolling in the Village begin to arrive. The place itself is so inviting on a beautiful summer evening that it looks like you are joining a party that started hours before. The gelato choices are so varied and the flavors so special it is hard to choose just one—and, happily, you don't have to. The size of the cup you choose is the only factor that limits the number of flavors you can select. Amorino's signature ice cream cone looks like a flower. Choose three flavors and then watch as this gorgeous ice cream flower is sculpted before your eyes. If you're so inclined, try the specialty called *focaccina*: a brioche-type cake sliced in half and filled with your choice of gelato. Or try a huge, crispy waffle with gelato and whipped cream, topped with fresh berries or granita. And if you don't want to have gelato, well, never mind, because there are many other choices, beginning with blended ice drinks and delicious milk shakes, then progressing to coffee, tea, and a piece of chocolate to top it all off. Everything at Amorino is organic and natural, without a single artificial morsel in anything served. As you step through the doors, it is easy to imagine you are somewhere in Italy, and after tasting the flavors, such as *stracciatella, cioccolato,* Caffè Altura, and Arancia Rossa, your taste buds might convince you that you are.

60 UNIVERSITY
PLACE
NEW YORK, NY
10003
212-253-5599
....
AMORINO.COM

NEW YORK SWEETS

AMY'S BREAD

THE QUINTESSENTIAL NEW YORK BAKERY

The Village
250 BLEECKER
STREET
NEW YORK, NY
10014
212-675-7802
....

Hell's Kitchen
672 NINTH AVE.
NEW YORK, NY
10036
212-977-2670
....

**Chelsea
Market**
75 NINTH AVE.
NEW YORK, NY
10011
212-462-4338
....

AMYSBREAD.COM

Amy Schreiber knows how to bake, having trained at the New York Restaurant School and Bouley Bakery. Qualifications do not come better than that, and neither does Amy's wonderful selection of pastries, cookies, old-fashioned layer cakes, cupcakes, brownies, bars, and biscotti. Amy believes in making carefully handcrafted foods that taste as good as they look. The products are all baked with natural ingredients and no artificial additives. Although I have visited all of the Amy's Bread locations and each is unique and inviting in its own way, the one on Bleecker Street is my favorite. There is something about the neighborhood ambience and the cheerful employees who are always smiling and saying hello. You are immediately drawn to the lusciously iced cakes on the countertop. The colors are eye-catching and the swirls of icing can make your mouth water. Fortunately, the cakes can be bought by the slice, but if you wish for the whole cake and nothing but the whole cake, that can be arranged, too. The Monkey Cake is for those who love a dense and fruity cake made with fresh bananas, pineapples, and toasted pecans—and, of course, topped with cream cheese frosting. If that does not whet your appetite, you can always try the traditional (and heavenly) red velvet cake, the angel food cake with lemon glaze, the Definitely Devil's Food Cake, the German chocolate cake, or the Black and White cake, which is my all-time favorite. Grab a pastry for breakfast, a slice of cake for tea, and a lime bar with coconut cream topping or one of the ginormous cookies to keep you satisfied in between. Whatever you choose, it will be memorable, and you might as well get to know the staff by name, since every customer becomes a regular.

NEW YORK SWEETS
....

BLACK OLIVE TWIST

...OLINA RAISIN ...ENNEL TWIST

WHOLE WHEAT FIVE GRAIN TWIST

$1.25

FRESH... AND ...

WHOLE WHEAT WALNUT TWIST

$1.50

ORGANIC WHOLE WHEAT, OAT, PECAN AND GOLDEN RAISIN TWIST

$1.50

...RY CREAM ...CONES $3.75

OAT SCONES WITH FIGS AND HAZELNUTS $3.25

...CHEESE AN... ...SCONE ...25

...$2.95

PUMPKIN CRANBERRY & WALNUT MUFFINS $2.95

ZUCCHINI, CARROT, APPLE AND WALNUT MUFFINS $2.95

OAT SCONES WITH FIGS AND HAZELNUTS $3.25

...SCONES $3.75

...DONUTS

...$1.50

ALMOND...

...BISCUITS ...1.35

CHEESE BISCUITS $1.50

WHOLE WHEAT BISCUITS $1.50

IRISH SODA BREAD WEDGE $2.25 RING $10.00

...WHEAT ...DA BREAD ...$2.25 ...$10.00

STICKY BUNS $2.95

BUTTERSCOTCH CASHEW BARS

NO NUT BROWNIES

ORNAMENTS

BROWNIES

You might as well get to know the staff by name, since every customer becomes a regular.

DON'T MISS:
Pretzel Croissant,
Rice Milk Muffin

raspberry
bran muffin
$3⁵⁰

Birdbath
cookies
$3

BIRDBATH

THE LITTLE SISTER TAKES OFF

A six-day pastry course in 1986 changed Maury Rubin's life. The former two-time Emmy Award–winning producer and director established City Bakery on Eighteenth Street in 1990. Maury is always reinventing himself, and he did so again with Birdbath, City Bakery's "little sister." The location on Prince Street is my favorite simply because I live nearby and had always gone to the now-shuttered and much-missed Vesuvio Bakery, an iconic coal-oven bread shop. When it closed, it seemed everyone in the neighborhood wondered what would take its place, and luckily Birdbath arrived. Maury kept the old bakery's sign and nearly everything else, green awning included. For me, Birdbath's muffins and scones are the superior choices—they're crisp on the outside and moist on the inside. My favorite is the Rice Milk Muffin with Red Beans and Ginger, which is an entire breakfast unto itself, but you can't go wrong with the cookie selection, either: the chocolate chip, oatmeal raisin, ginger, peanut butter, and white chocolate chip varieties are all outstanding. City Bakery and Birdbath are both well known for their pretzel croissant, and I recommend enjoying the crumbly, chewy, salty, flaky, crispy, sesame-covered treat dunked in your morning coffee. No doubt you will want to savor it, so you might as well call in late for work even before you order one.

SoHo
160 PRINCE STREET
NEW YORK, NY
10012
646-556-7720
....
East Village
223 FIRST AVE.
NEW YORK, NY
10003
646-722-6565
....
35 THIRD AVENUE
NEW YORK, NY
10003
212-201-1902
....
Tribeca
200 CHURCH STREET
NEW YORK, NY
10013
212-309-7555
....
New Museum
235 BOWERY
NEW YORK, NY
10002
212-219-1222
....
THECITYBAKERY.COM/
BIRDBATH

BOSIE TEA PARLOR
IMAGINATIVE DELICACIES

In 2010, Kiley Holliday and Nicky Dawda opened the Bosie Tea Parlor, a cozy, delightful restaurant and bakery on Morton Street in the heart of New York City's West Village. Pastry chef Damien Herrgott served at Ladurée Royale and Pierre Hermé in Paris before moving stateside to work at Bouley Bakery and then Bosie. Gourmands flock here to partake in the delightful ritual of morning or afternoon tea, and they linger as they try their second and sometimes third imaginative delicacy. The Ispahan is an exquisitely crafted rose *macaron* filled with rose buttercream, lychee, and fresh raspberries. Bosie boasts a wall of exotic teas from around the world, and Chef Herrgott enjoys using them in his pastries. The Mille Crepe is made with Earl Grey cream sandwiched between layers of thin crepes, and the Darjeeling Tart features sweet dough, Darjeeling ganache, *crème Chantilly*, and nougat. My favorite is the Victoria (coconut dacquoise, coconut cream, and pineapple, seasoned with lime zest, cilantro, and black pepper), but any pastry you choose will leave you wide-eyed—and the *macarons* might even make you weep.

HARNEY & SONS
A DIFFERENT KIND OF BREWHOUSE

John Harney is the patriarch of the Harney family and the president and founder of Harney & Sons, a family company established in 1983 and devoted to the tradition of tea. Masters of tea blending, Harney & Sons is one of the world's most renowned tea companies, with more than two hundred gourmet teas on offer, sourced from China, Taiwan, India, Sri Lanka, Africa, and Japan. The Harney tradition of tea is simple—to make great tea an everyday luxury. Harney & Sons opened its SoHo tearoom in 2010, providing a Zen-like atmosphere for tasting tea and an education in the subject that you won't soon forget. The wall of shelves filled with tins of loose teas from around the world and their matching exotic names will give you pause for thought. The teas, the brewing paraphernalia, the sachets, the iced teas, and the friendly tutelage of the staff ensure that even if you weren't a tea drinker when you entered the store, you certainly will be by the time you leave it. John Harney continues to serve as the quintessential brand ambassador and "tea-vangelist," spreading the everyday enjoyment of tea to the masses.

BOSIENYC.COM
10 MORTON STREET ~ NEW YORK, NY 10014 ~ 212-352-9900

HARNEY.COM
433 BROOME STREET ~ NEW YORK, NY 10013 ~ 212-933-4853

JACQUES TORRES CHOCOLATE
THE WILLY WONKA OF NEW YORK

From the huge windows on Hudson Street, you can watch the chocolatiers at work mixing huge vats of the stuff, and if that does not urge you to enter, then the intoxicating aromas of the chocolate sure will. This is no ordinary chocolate shop. It's one full of skill, imagination, and fun. It comes as no surprise that Jacques Torres is known as Mr. Chocolate. Brought up in France, he originally trained as a pastry chef, but his passion for chocolate led him to become an artisan chocolatier, and he began making his own chocolate, from cocoa beans to finished confection. The products contain no preservatives and all of the chocolates are handmade with the purest ingredients available. The store has a wide selection, starting with champagne truffles and continuing with bars, barks, and chocolates in assorted boxes. It seems Torres will cover almost anything with chocolate, including marshmallows, raisins, nuts, espresso beans, Cheerios, and cornflakes, and then wrap it up beautifully before it is enjoyed.

MRCHOCOLATE.COM
HUDSON STREET 350 HUDSON STREET ∾ NY, NY 10014 ∾ 212-414-2462
AMSTERDAM AVENUE 285 AMSTERDAM AVE. ∾ NY, NY 10023 ∾ 212-787-3256
DUMBO 66 WATER STREET ∾ BROOKLYN, NY 11201 ∾ 718-875-1269
ROCKEFELLER CENTER 30 ROCKEFELLER PLAZA ∾ CONCOURSE LEVEL ∾
NY, NY 10112 ∾ 212-664-1804
ICE CREAM SHOP 62 WATER STREET ∾ BROOKLYN, NY 11201 ∾ 718-875-1269
CHELSEA MARKET 75 NINTH AVE. ∾ NY, NY 10011 ∾ 212-229-2241

PASTICCERIA ROCCO
REAL OLD-SCHOOL CHARACTER

Rocco's is *the* place to go for authentic Italian pastries in Greenwich Village. The bakery has been in the family since 1974, and current head pastry chef Rocco Generoso Jr. certainly got the baking gene. The enormous cookie display in the window will make your eyes go wide, but you can't go wrong no matter what you choose. Famous for its cannoli, filled fresh before your eyes and dotted with chocolate chips, Rocco's also has a vast selection of miniature pastries, biscotti, and cakes. The best way to navigate your way around the myriad sweets is to arrive with a group of friends who like to share as much as they like to indulge in treats. The éclair is an explosion of cream and chocolate, but my favorite is the biscotti, which come with either pecans and dried cranberries, chocolate and almonds, or candied fruit. Rocco's is filled with genuine character (and, sometimes, characters!), and it's easy to enjoy this throwback to the *Godfather* era.

PASTICCERIAROCCO.COM
243 BLEECKER STREET ∾ NEW YORK, NY 10014 ∾ 212-242-6031

DEAN & DELUCA
THE EMPORIUM THAT STARTED IT ALL

Dean & DeLuca first opened in SoHo in 1977. At the time, the gourmet-food movement was in its early days, and there weren't all that many stores where the average person could buy food items from around the world. The store is by now a veritable theme park of every kind of food imaginable, but the sweets deserve particular notice. Although the store sources many of its pastries from some of the best bakers in New York City, Dean & DeLuca has a mean patisserie all its own. There are chocolates in many sizes, shapes, and permutations, as well as cupcakes, pies, brownies, tarts, and whoopie pies. All adorn glass cabinets, arrayed on cake platters, just waiting to be chosen and devoured. The sheer amount of whipped cream, frosting, chocolate chips, peanut butter, marshmallows, dried fruits, and nuts on display—not to mention the giant jars full of licorice, hard candies, soft candies, gummies, chewies, and crunchies—makes it quite difficult to choose. George Bernard Shaw wrote, "There is no love sincerer than the love of food," and it's clear that this store not only loves food but also champions its customers' love of the same. Walk through the doors of Dean & DeLuca and fall in love.

CHOCOLATE LACE
COOKIES
$30/LB

AMY'S
KEY LIME
$30/LB

ALFAJORES
$3.50

NUT B

TATTE FINE CAKES
NUT BOX
MIXED NUTS WITH CARAMELIZED
FILLING
$8

SETTEPANI
AMARETTI
$30/LB

SETTEPANI BAKE
PIGNOLI

AMY'S
COOKIE
$5

WONDERFULLY MADE CAKES
LEMON RASPBERRY
CUPCAKE
MEYER LEMON CAKE WITH FRES
RASPBERRY BUTTERCREAM

$4.50

Walk through the
doors of Dean & DeLuca
and fall in love.

SEA SAL
LICORIC
HOLLAND

NEY LICORIC

RASPBERRY
KOOKABURRA
AUSTRALIA $9/LB

MANGO
KOOKABURRA
AUSTRALIA $9/L

RICE ICE
$9/LB

GRANDAISY BAKERY

AN AMERICAN BAKERY WITH ITALIAN ROOTS

Formerly the Sullivan Street Bakery, this sweet destination was renamed Grandaisy Bakery by owner Monica Von Thun Calderón (in honor of her grandmother Daisy), and it's simply one of the best European bakeries in New York City. Brush up on your Italian and ask for a Tortino di Carotta—you will soon be munching on a miniature carrot cake. Select the Torte Grandaisy, an almond pound cake with citrus essence, or the Budino di Pane, a bread pudding made with brioche croissant and dripping in caramel. The bakery uses local and seasonal produce, so the menu changes often, but no bakery would be complete without a chocolate cake, and Grandaisy's practically melts before your eyes. If fruit is your thing, try the strawberry-and-rhubarb tart, any of the fruit turnovers, the banana-walnut pullman loaf, or any of the pullmans made using seasonal fruits. The shop is well known for its biscotti: Americani are rich, buttery treats made with chocolate chips and hazelnuts, and the Zenzeri are gingersnaps spiced so perfectly that you won't be able to stop yourself at only one. My favorite is the Ossi di Morti, made of meringue and sugared almonds: white clouds of decadence! Once you have tried Grandaisy's treats, like a bloodhound you will make your way back for your daily fix.

Tribeca
250 W. BROADWAY
NEW YORK, NY
10013
212-334-9435
....
Upper West Side
176 W. 72ND STREET
NEW YORK, NY
10023
212-334-9435
....
GRANDAISY
BAKERY.COM

IL CANTUCCIO
BISCOTTI BEYOND WORDS

91 CHRISTOPHER
STREET
NEW YORK, NY
10014
212-647-8787
....
ILCANTUCCIONYC.COM

Since the mid-1990s, Lorenzo Palombo and Simone Bertini, childhood friends who grew up together near Florence, wanted to open a New York City outpost for their Italian bakery. The duo already had two shops in Italy, one in Florence and another in Migliana, a small village nearby. The bakery became well known for its *cantucci*, a colloquial name for biscotti, almond cookies, and the like.

A third friend, Camilla Bottari, joined them, and Il Cantuccio opened on Christopher Street in the West Village in 2009. Palombo carries on the tradition of baking the amazing biscotti with a recipe that has been used—and guarded—since 1940. The *cantucci* are made with flour, sugar, eggs, almonds, and pine nuts, but the real treasures for your taste buds are the various fillings. Choose among almond, apricot, dark chocolate, prune, and figs. The soft texture and choice of fillings give new meaning to the word *biscotti*, since they come out of the oven moist and chewy. The chocolate variety with a cappuccino is beyond words. I usually leave with a few *bruttiboni*, cookies made of almonds ground finely into a paste, and some Nutella focaccia, but my very favorite is the Pan di Ramerini, a sweet yet savory bread filled to bursting with raisins and rosemary. As they say: When in Rome, do as the Romans do. And that's easy to do here.

KEE'S CHOCOLATES
A ONE-WOMAN MACHINE

Kee's was founded by Kee Lee Tong in 2002, after she quit her corporate job and followed her dream of making handmade chocolates. A small woman with the hands of a diamond setter, Kee makes thousands of pieces of her irresistible chocolate every week. She's the inventive genius behind everything. She creates the recipes, mixes the chocolate, makes the molds, stocks the displays, and serves the customers. Seven days a week, Kee can be found at her dollhouse-sized shop making fresh chocolates. Kee uses only fresh ingredients, and she sources them from around the world, including *yuzu* from Japan, sea salt from France, and saffron from Spain. On a visit to the store, I watched her pour the silky chocolate into molds and pop them out with the agility of a seasoned juggler. Luckily for me, I even got to taste a few. My favorites out of the fifty or so flavors on offer are the cherry cordial, the honey kumquat, the dark chocolate with ginger, the dark chocolate coconut truffle, and the passion fruit heart. The special touch of the artisan is what makes Kee's Chocolates a definite stop on any visit to SoHo.

SoHo
80 THOMPSON
STREET
NEW YORK, NY
10012
212-334-3284
....
Midtown
452 FIFTH AVE.
(INSIDE HSBC)
NEW YORK, NY
10018
212-525-6099
....
315 WEST 39TH
STREET
NEW YORK, NY
10018
212-967-8088
....
KEESCHOCOLATES.
COM

MAGNOLIA BAKERY

WHERE IT ALL STARTED

When Alyssa Torey opened Magnolia Bakery in 1996, she had no idea that she would be at the center of a cupcake phenomenon that would sweep the country. With its vintage American desserts and 1950s decor, Magnolia was conceived as a way to step back in time and kick back with a treat and a cup of coffee. With this idea in her mind and a small loan from her father in her pocket, she transformed a run-down Bleecker Street storefront into a neighborhood hot spot and a tourist attraction for travelers from all around the world. Soon after opening, the cupcakes garnered buzz and lines started forming. Then it was featured on HBO's New York City-centric show *Sex and the City*, and the place's popularity boomed. Perpetually and exceptionally long lines were the new normal for the bakery. The desserts, frankly, deserve the attention. Magnolia bakes everything from scratch with all-natural ingredients and no preservatives. The simple vanilla and chocolate cupcakes topped with buttercream icing in chocolate, vanilla, and pastel colors are practically worthy of an Oscar, and certainly of the cultish following they induce. The luscious cakes (basically, bigger versions of the cupcakes) are piled high with gooey icing. The coconut layer cake is laced with coconut filling and topped with meringue icing, the Hummingbird cake features bananas, pineapple, and pecans, and the devil's food cake is made with Dutch cocoa and a choice of chocolate, caramel, or mocha buttercream frosting. And although Magnolia is best known for its cupcakes, it also offers cookies, bars, brownies, fruit crisps, and pies. In 2007, Alyssa decided to pass her toque to a new family, who have expanded Magnolia's reach—there are now multiple locations throughout the city—but kept the same recipes and integrity of the products.

Bleecker Street
401 BLEECKER ST.
NEW YORK, NY 10014
212-462-2572
....

Columbus Ave.
200 COLUMBUS AVE.
NEW YORK, NY
10023
212-724-8101
....

Grand Central Terminal
LOWER LEVEL
DINING CONCOURSE
212-682-3588
....

Bloomingdale's
1000 THIRD AVE.
NEW YORK, NY
10022
212-265-5320
....

Rockefeller Center
1240 AVENUE OF
THE AMERICAS
NEW YORK, NY
10020
212-767-1123
....

MAGNOLIA
BAKERY.COM

Strawberry Ice Box Cake

MAKES 1 (7- OR 8-INCH) CAKE; 8 SERVINGS

FROM THE KITCHEN OF MAGNOLIA BAKERY

1 QUART HEAVY CREAM

2 TABLESPOONS SUGAR

1¼ CUPS STRAWBERRY PUREE

1 RECIPE CHOCOLATE WAFERS (RECIPE FOLLOWS), OR ABOUT 100 STORE-BOUGHT NABISCO CHOCOLATE WAFER COOKIES

CHOCOLATE WAFERS

1½ CUPS SUGAR

1¼ CUPS ALL-PURPOSE FLOUR

½ CUP UNSWEETENED DUTCH-PROCESS COCOA POWDER

1 TEASPOON BAKING SODA

¼ TEASPOON BAKING POWDER

¼ TEASPOON SALT

10 TABLESPOONS UNSALTED BUTTER

1 LARGE EGG

1. Put the cream in the bowl of a stand mixer fitted with the whisk attachment. With the mixer on low speed, slowly pour in the sugar. Increase the speed to medium-high and whip until the cream thickens slightly in the middle. Increase the speed to high and whip for 30 seconds to 1 minute, until the cream is very thick.

2. Remove the mixer bowl from the stand; gently add the strawberry puree, folding it into the whipped cream with a rubber spatula until fully combined. *Do not stir the whipped cream or whip it in the mixer again.*

3. Place an 8-inch doily on a cardboard cake round or plate set on a lazy susan. Using an offset spatula, spread a very thin layer of cream on the doily, spinning and smoothing the cream out to the inner edge of the doily. Use just enough cream for the first layer of wafers to stick to the doily.

4. Place 7 wafer cookies around the edge of the whipped cream and one in the center.

5. Be sure the wafers are equal distance from one another.

6. Place about ½ cup of the whipped cream in the center for your first layer. Using the offset spatula, smooth the cream out almost out to the edge until you can barely see the edges of the wafers.

7. For the second layer, use 7 more cookies, placing them directly in between the first layer of wafers, making sure they are equal distance from one another. Continue making layers of whipped cream and wafers, stacking the cookies like bricks (for example, the third layer of wafers will be placed directly on top of the first layer of wafers), until the cake is 10 to 12 layers high.

8. Put in a Tupperware cake container and chill in the refrigerator for 5 to 6 hours before serving.

CHOCOLATE WAFERS

1. Preheat the oven to 275°F.

2. Put the sugar, flour, cocoa powder, baking soda, baking powder, and salt in a food processor.

3. Add the butter and pulse to combine. Add the egg and continue to pulse until thoroughly combined.

4. Divide the dough into two equal portions, flatten each into a disc, wrap in plastic, and refrigerate until firm.

5. Roll out the dough on a lightly floured work surface until paper thin, then cut out 2-inch circles. Reroll the scraps and cut more circles. Place the circles on baking sheets and bake for 8 to 10 minutes, until crisp. Remove to wire racks to cool completely.

Sweets Sampler: Chocolate Chip Cookies

IS THERE ANYTHING MORE COMFORTING THAN A CHOCOLATE CHIP COOKIE, fresh from the oven, with a cold glass of milk? They are a hugely satisfying treat. Thin and crispy or thick and chewy, you can find them in New York in all sizes and with additions that range from caramel to peanut butter to cornflakes.

CHOCOLATE CHIP COOKIE

CORNFLAKE CHOCOLATE CHIP MARSHMALLOW COOKIE

CHOCOLATE CHIP WALNUT COOKIE

BIRDBATH // PG 17
Large enough to be crunchy on the outside and thick and chewy on the inside, this one is a classic. It's big enough that you think you can share it with a friend, but a word of advice: You won't want to.

MOMOFUKU MILK BAR // PG 87
The twist here is the addition of marshmallow and cornflakes to your standard chocolate chip cookie. Oh, what a difference it makes! It's wonderfully chewy with great butter flavor.

LEVAIN BAKERY // PG 130
This is a supersized cookie, thick and mounded. It has a crunchy exterior but that rounded dome hides a fantastically gooey, doughy interior. Every bite resonates with chocolate and walnut flavor.

MILK CHOCOLATE CARAMEL COOKIE

CHOCOLATE CHIP PEANUT BUTTER COOKIE

CHOCOLATE CHIP COOKIE

MILK & COOKIES BAKERY // OPPOSITE
Mild, very sweet, and doughy, this cookie is a gorgeous butterscotch brown in color. It's cooked just past raw on the inside, but has some crunch along the outer rim.

JACQUES TORRES CHOCOLATE // PG 19
The peanut flavor comes out strong in these cookies, balanced by big hunks of chocolate and a thick, cakelike texture.

OLIVE'S // PG 35
This is a chewy and moist cookie, with thin layers of chocolate chunk laced throughout.

MILK & COOKIES BAKERY

PURE COMFORT IN SMALL PACKAGES

Tucked away on Commerce Street in the West Village is Milk & Cookies. Owner Tina Casaceli, owing to her education at, variously, the Culinary Institute, some of the best restaurants in New York City, and her grandmother's knee, gives new meaning to the word cookie. Her creations are complex, they're made with the best ingredients, and they come out of the oven fresh all day long. The aroma of the freshly baked cookies alone is enough to lead you down Commerce Street and directly to the shop. No matter what your cookie fancy, you will find it here and then some. The choices include chocolate chip (of course), oatmeal raisin, Salted Oat Surprise, Bacon Smack, dark chocolate toffee, s'mores, and white chocolate macadamia. And forget those store-bought ice cream sandwiches—Tina's are the real deal. Try the Sugar Bomb (sugar cookies with the flavor of the week) or the Grasshopper (chocolate mint cookies with mint ice cream), among others. Tina believes there is nothing like a freshly baked warm cookie to put a smile on your face and make you feel comforted. Personally, my face lights up at the thought of the white chocolate cherry oatmeal cookies. While you're there, you might as well buy one of her mixes so you can make your own warm cookies at home.

19 COMMERCE
STREET
NEW YORK, NY
10014
212-243-1640
....

MILKANDCOOKIES
BAKERY.COM

Oatmeal-Raisin Cookies

MAKES 24 COOKIES

FROM THE KITCHEN OF MILK & COOKIES BAKERY

1½ CUPS ALL-PURPOSE FLOUR

1 TABLESPOON GROUND CINNAMON

1 TEASPOON BAKING SODA

½ TEASPOON SALT

1½ CUPS (3 STICKS) UNSALTED BUTTER, AT ROOM TEMPERATURE

1 CUP FIRMLY PACKED LIGHT BROWN SUGAR

½ CUP GRANULATED SUGAR

2 LARGE EGGS, AT ROOM TEMPERATURE

1 TABLESPOON PURE VANILLA EXTRACT

3 CUPS OLD-FASHIONED ROLLED OATS

1½ CUPS RAISINS

1. Preheat the oven to 350°F. Line two baking sheets with silicone baking mats or parchment paper.

2. Combine the flour, cinnamon, baking soda, and salt in a bowl. Set aside.

3. Put the butter in the bowl of a stand mixer fitted with the paddle attachment. Begin beating on low speed. Add the sugars. Increase the speed to medium and beat for about 4 minutes, until light and creamy.

4. Add the eggs, one at a time, and beat to incorporate, scraping down the sides of the bowl with a rubber spatula after each addition.

5. Beat in the vanilla, then gradually mix in the flour mixture and oats; do not overmix the dough or the cookies will be dry and hard—stop while the dough is still streaky and remove the bowl from the mixer.

6. Scrape the dough onto a lightly floured work surface. Lightly flour your hands and finish mixing the dough by using a gentle kneading motion, working until the dry ingredients are just incorporated. Using a wooden spoon, stir in the raisins, mixing until evenly distributed.

7. Using a tablespoon or small ice-cream scoop, make balls of dough, then roll into balls about 1½ inches in diameter. Place the balls about 2 inches apart on the prepared baking sheets. Using your palm, gently flatten the top of each cookie slightly. Bake for about 15 minutes, until lightly browned around the edges. The center should be slightly soft to the touch. Using a metal spatula, transfer the cookies to wire racks to cool. Store in an airtight container at room temperature for up to 1 week.

DON'T MISS:
Morning Buns, Jessie's Cowgirl Cookie, and Sarah's Brownie

941 - 0111
Take Out
Delivery
Catering

OLIVE'S
AN ANCHOR OF THE NEIGHBORHOOD

At one time, SoHo was an artist's haven, its warehouses suitable for studios, not commerce. Now it is as crowded as any neighborhood in the city, with visitors from all over the world. Husband-and-wife team Nick Hartman and Tony Allocca opened Olive's in 1992 on Prince Street with a mission to provide the people living in the area with delicious, freshly prepared foods to take on the go. These days, the line starts early in the morning for the freshly baked croissants, pain au chocolate, muffins, scones, and the famous Morning Buns—sticky buns that are gooey beyond belief and finger-licking fantastic. The fruit salad overflows with berries, mangoes, watermelon, pineapple, papaya, grapes, and kiwi—a fruit market in a cup!. But the main event is the homemade cookies. The crisp but chewy chocolate chip cookies are so full of chips that each bite drips with chocolate. Other flavors include oatmeal raisin, oatmeal pecan, peanut butter, and ginger. The Jessie's Cowgirl cookie is my favorite—full of dark and white chocolate, as well as dried cherries. Sarah's Brownie, chock-full of walnuts, is a decadent treat. And, so your dog doesn't feel left out, Olive's also has cookies for canines. Olive's has some of the best cookies in town—and their regular menu is pretty terrific, too!

120 PRINCE STREET
NEW YORK, NY
10012
212-941-0111
....
OLIVESNYC.COM

ONCE UPON A TART...

A HIDDEN JEWELBOX

135 SULLIVAN
STREET
NEW YORK, NY
10012
212-387-8869
....

ONCEUPONA
TART.COM

Jerome Audureau opened Once Upon a Tart... on Sullivan Street in SoHo two decades ago, and it is still going strong. From the old oak doors to the old-timey feel to the freshly baked pastries, the place is a crowd pleaser. Locals duly arrive in the morning for coffee and the signature scones and muffins. Audureau also bakes sweet tarts, which resemble miniature pies, fresh daily. Big glass jars filled with various flavors of tempting biscotti are great for dipping in a hot cup of coffee. So what will it be? Choose among the items already mentioned or try a brownie, a madeleine, a macaroon, or a cookie. My favorite is a slice of iced carrot cake because I always end up licking the icing from the end of my fingers, like I did when I was a kid. Once Upon a Tart... adds a new dimension to the world of gastronomic sweets, and it's so good that once you discover it, well, you might just want to keep it to yourself.

FRANCOIS PAYARD BAKERY

A LEGENDARY FRENCH MASTER

François Payard is a James Beard Award–winning pastry chef who grew up in the French Riviera town of Nice learning the techniques of classic French pastry at an early age in his grandfather's shop. Many years, four-star ratings, and culinary awards later, he opened Payard Patisserie in 1997. In 2010, he moved from that original, much loved Upper East Side location to SoHo and christened the new spot FPB (short for Francois Payard Bakery). As you might imagine from such an esteemed chef, the breakfast pastries are in a league of their own. The classic French morning breads—butter croissants, almond croissants, and pain au chocolate—will give you an idea of what the man is all about. The scones and muffins will impress the most demanding of customers, and the pastries and tarts, which look almost too good to eat, taste as exquisite as they look. The signature cake selection includes Le Gâteau Roulé, a light rolled cake in flavors like chocolate-raspberry, milk chocolate espresso, hazelnut, and cheesecake passion fruit. Or try the French version of angel food cake called Le Lorrain. Payard's Croquembouche, a tower of profiteroles filled with vanilla, chocolate, coffee, kirsch, or vanilla rhum cream and finished with hand-pulled sugar ribbons, is nothing less than legendary. The colorful *macarons* are presented like jewels in a box, and the handmade chocolates and truffles are out of this world. My favorite is the flourless chocolate cookies: large, fudgy, crispy, and filled with walnuts. He has dreamed up sweet creations to please palates at locations in New York City and throughout the world, and for his efforts you will surely leave saying, "*Merci beaucoup*, Monsieur Payard!"

Greenwich Village
116 WEST HOUSTON STREET
NEW YORK, NY
10012
212-995-0888
. . . .
Columbus Circle
1775 BROADWAY
NEW YORK, NY
10019
212-956-1775
. . . .
Battery Park
210 MURRAY STREET
NEW YORK, NY
10282
212-566-8300
. . . .
Midtown
THE PLAZA HOTEL
1 WEST 58TH STREET
NEW YORK, NY
10019
212-759-1603
. . . .
PAYARD.COM

Flourless Chocolate Cookies

MAKES 12 (4-INCH) COOKIES

FROM THE KITCHEN OF FRANCOIS PAYARD BAKERY

½ CUP PLUS 3 TABLESPOONS UNSWEETENED DUTCH-PROCESS COCOA POWDER

3 CUPS CONFECTIONERS' SUGAR

PINCH OF SALT

2¾ CUPS WALNUTS, TOASTED AND COARSELY CHOPPED

4 LARGE EGG WHITES, AT ROOM TEMPERATURE

1 TABLESPOON PURE VANILLA EXTRACT

1. Preheat the oven to 350°F and place racks in the upper and lower thirds of the oven. Line two baking sheets with parchment paper or silicone baking mats.

2. Combine the cocoa powder, confectioners' sugar, salt, and walnuts in the bowl of an electric mixer fitted with the paddle attachment. Mix on low speed for 1 minute.

3. With the mixer running, gradually add the egg whites and vanilla. Mix on medium speed for 3 minutes, until the mixture has thickened slightly; do not overmix, or the egg whites will thicken too much.

4. With a 2-ounce cookie or ice cream scoop or a large spoon, scoop the dough onto the prepared baking sheets to make cookies that are 4 inches in diameter; scoop 5 cookies onto each pan, about 3 inches apart so that they don't stick to one another when they spread. If you have extra dough, wait until the first batch of cookies is baked before scooping the next batch.

5. Put the cookies in the oven and immediately lower the oven temperature to 320°F.

6. Bake for 14 to 16 minutes, or until small, thin cracks appear on the surface of the cookies, switching the pans halfway through.

7. Pull the parchment paper with the cookies onto a wire rack and let cool completely before removing the cookies from the paper. Store in an airtight container for up to 2 days.

Sweets Sampler: Scones

OUR FAVORITE BREAKFAST-ON-THE-RUN, the ideal scone is tender and flaky. It's the biscuit's slightly sweeter cousin. Too often they are dry and heavy, but not the ones below.

MIXED BERRY SCONE

BIRDBATH // PG 17
This scone is loaded with berries, and has really balanced flavor and the perfect amount of moistness and sugar.

CHOCOLATE CHUNK SCONE

CLINTON ST. BAKING COMPANY // PG 67
This scone has a crunchy textured exterior, a moist interior, and giant chunks of dark chocolate.

AMY'S CHERRY CREAM SCONE

AMY'S BREAD // PG 14
Its large sprawling shape makes it all American, but this rendition honors the scone's traditional British roots by using real cream in the dough.

EXPLODED SCONE

BOSIE TEA PARLOR // PG 18
This is a simple scone, elevated to five-star dessert, with raspberry jam in the center and perfectly garnished with icing on top.

OATMEAL RAISIN SCONE

LEVAIN BAKERY // PG 130
A hearty and flavorful scone, studded with golden raisins, is not too sweet and manages to be light despite the oatmeal.

FIG AND APPLE SCONE

BAKERI // PG 153
A giant flat triangle, this scone has a super crunchy top thanks to oats and streusel, with big moist chunks of fresh apple below. It's substantial but light in texture.

RON BEN-ISRAEL CAKES

CAKES TO DIE FOR

42 GREENE STREET
NEW YORK, NY
10013
212-625-3369
....

WEDDINGCAKES.COM

Ron Ben-Israel grew up with a fascination for baking because, thanks to his Viennese mother and her extensive baking skills, he witnessed the transformation of ordinary ingredients into cakes, strudels, and meringues. Following a stint in the Israeli army, he went to fine art school to study set design, and soon after that became a professional dancer. When he could no longer ignore the siren song of the kitchen, he served several apprenticeships in France and then opened Ron Ben-Israel Cakes in SoHo. Christened "the Manolo Blahnik of wedding cakes" by the *New York Times*, he's the go-to guy for those in the know when an occasion calls for a custom-made cake. After a consultation and tasting session with Ron, you will realize that the business of making cakes is serious and detailed. The artisans at this pristine facility make every element of every design by hand. Ron has invented cake categories that include Romance, Bold Statements, Graphics & Textures, Lace & Beading, For Him, For Her, and Good Times, among others, and he caters for all tastes, including making cakes that are kosher, or dairy-, lactose-, gluten-, or sugar-free. As he often intones on his popular Food Network show, *Sweet Genius*, "Let your imagination run wild" as you plan your cake, because anything you can imagine can become reality with this sweet genius behind the oven.

"Let your imagination run wild" as you plan your cake, because anything you can imagine can become reality with this sweet genius behind the oven.

SANT AMBROEUS

LA DOLCE VITA

The original Sant Ambroeus, named after the patron saint of Milan, opened its doors in Milan, Italy, in 1936. It soon became an important meeting place for the local intelligentsia. Three generations later, on West 4th Street and on Madison Avenue in New York City, Sant Ambroeus is still an important meeting place, and when you walk inside it is easy to see why. The place exudes old-world charm, the conversation is hushed, and the pastries, cookies, and cakes are in perfect presentation. The restaurant remains true to its heritage in every way, from the staff speaking Italian to the design and, of course, the pastries and gelato. Start the day with a cappuccino and a cornetti, a walnut twist with apricot jam or vanilla cream raisin, or a sugar brioche. I always marvel at how the butter cookies are placed with utmost care, one by one, into a package that is then wrapped in paper and tied with a bow. I call it this process the "cookie ceremony." But for the cake lovers among you, the Sant Ambroeus is famous for *la dolce vita*: a chocolate custard–filled chocolate mousse cake. There are gorgeous seasonal tarts, all sorts of pastries, assorted gelato flavors, and, my favorite, the Nocciola: hazelnut sponge cake with hazelnut buttercream and caramelized salted almonds. Italian at its best!

West Village
259 WEST 4TH
STREET
NEW YORK, NY
10014
212-604-9254
....
**Madison
Avenue**
1000 MADISON AVE.
NEW YORK, NY
10021
212-570-2211
....
SANTAMBROEUS.COM

SOCKERBIT

SMORGASBORD OF SWEETS

89 CHRISTOPHER
STREET
NEW YORK, NY
10014
212-206-8170

....

SOCKERBIT.COM

Sockerbit, which means "sugar cube" in Swedish, is a store full of just that, and so much more: jellies, gummies, chewy things, sticky things, gooey things, rolled things, crunchy things, and mushy things, in just about every shape, size, flavor, and color you can imagine. The candies, which are housed in clear drawers that line an entire wall of this bright and extraordinarily alluring shop on Christopher Street in the West Village, appear with detailed descriptions, so even though the sweets are Swedish, you don't have to guess what you're about to enjoy. The idea is that you compose your own bag of candy out of the more than one hundred choices (all of which are made with natural ingredients and food colors derived from nature). The owners, Stefan Ernberg, a Swede, and his wife, Florence Baras, an Argentinian, are as sweet as the things they sell, and they are clearly passionate about candy. They've succeeded in creating an inviting space where the center of attention is sweets, and their *smagodis* ("little candies") will give your sweet tooth a run for its money.

sockerbit®

Compose your own
bag of candy out
of the more than one
hundred choices.

KELVIN NATURAL SLUSH CO.
MAKING THE STREETS COOLER

What is a slush? When I was growing up, a slush was shaved ice in a cup with a funky sweet syrup. The ice cream man shaved the big block of ice that was sitting atop his cart into a cup and offered you a variety of candy-colored liquids to put on top. Kelvin Natural Slush Co.'s grown-up slush brings this process to a heightened level of excellence. These slushes are made with filtered water, cane sugar, and fresh fruit purees. Choose from ice flavors like Spicy Ginger, Tangy Citrus, or Green and Black Tea, and then add the magic toppings, choosing from a rotating selection that includes white peach, raspberry, guava, green apple, cherry, pear, blueberry, caramelized pineapple, and mango. The roving blue Kelvin truck roams the city with its mission to "make the streets of NYC a little cooler one slush at a time." It's hard to imagine anything more refreshing on a hot summer day.

L'ARTE DEL GELATO
A REAL GEM

Diamonds are a girl's best friend, but that was not enough to keep Francesco Realmuto and Salvatore Potestio working as cutters in New York City's Diamond District for long. The pair's shared passion for the perfect gelato led them to give up on gems and instead study the art of gelato in Italy. For their efforts, they were entrusted with secrets from the masters of the art and upon their return they opened L'Arte del Gelato in Chelsea Market in 2005. Everything is made fresh daily using only the best, purest ingredients sourced from all over the world: pistachios and olive oil from Sicily, hazelnuts from Italy, Valrhona chocolate from France. Their secret methodology produces a dense, full consistency but with less fat than ice creams. The refreshing fat-free sorbets come in flavors like lemon-orange, grape, and pear. Gelato flavors include chocolate with orange, banana, milk with sour cherries, peanut butter, *panna cotta*, and chocolate with rum. My favorite is the Affogato al Caffe: *vaniglia* with espresso and whipped cream.

LARTEDELGELATO.COM
WEST VILLAGE 75 7TH AVENUE SOUTH ∾ NY, NY 10014 ∾ 212-924-0803
CHELSEA MARKET 75 NINTH AVE. ∾ NY, NY 10011 ∾ 212-366-0570
LINCOLN CENTER PLAZA MAY TO AUGUST

KELVINSLUSH.COM
MULTIPLE LOCATIONS ∾ 646-200-5083

POPBAR
INVENTIVE FROZEN TREATS ON A STICK

The word is out on Popbar, and it has been since May 2010, when it opened. Pop into the store on Carmine Street in the West Village and you will soon know why it's such a popular place. The popGelato, popSorbetto, and YogurtPops served by the cheerful team in the fun atmosphere will turn you into a Popaholic on your first visit. If that thought worries you, then rest assured that the ingredients are pure, have no artificial colors or preservatives, and contain fresh fruit. The handmade popGelato (gelato on a stick) is made fresh daily, but the flavors change with the seasons. These include banana, chocolate, coffee, cream, and even gianduia, the hazelnut-flavored chocolate often found in truffles. The coconut popGelato with coconut shavings, dipped in premium dark chocolate, is on the decadent side, but the lighter and fruitier popSorbetto flavors include blood orange, grapefruit, lemon, mandarin orange, mixed berry, orange, peach, and mango. The YogurtPops, made with fresh fruit, come in either classic or strawberry flavors. Popbar allows you to add your personal touch to everything they sell, be it nuts of all kinds, granola, coffee grains, or sprinkles. Go on, pop into Popbar. It's positively popping!

POP-BAR.COM
5 CARMINE STREET ∾ NEW YORK, NY 10014 ∾ 212-255-4874

VICTORY GARDEN
SOFT-SERVE WITH A TWANG

Sophia Britten sowed the seeds for her future while she was enjoying a bowl of goat milk yogurt. Her culinary and nutritional background helped her realize there was a gap in the market for a goat milk yogurt, and from that notion, Victory Garden was born in 2011. The unassuming yet always packed shop serves goat milk soft-serve, with a regularly rotating roster of flavors. Chocolate, rose petal, lemon poppy, and coffee are always popular, but the best-seller is the delicious salted caramel. All of the ingredients are sourced locally. The goat milk comes from Beltane Farm in Lebanon, Connecticut, where the goats are fed hay and grass (and *not* antibiotics). Lactose-intolerant people can eat the product without worry, and it's a little healthier than regular yogurt in that it is lower in fat and also enriched with iron, calcium, protein, and potassium. Believe it or not, this is a food that is healthy and tastes great. Toppings include exotic treats like maple marshmallows and honeycomb candy, as well as pretzels and fresh seasonal fruits. A huge picture of a goat hangs on the wall, and its expression suggests it knows that what he has given us is as good as it gets.

VICTORYGARDENNYC.COM
31 CARMINE STREET ∾ NEW YORK, NY 10014 ∾ 212-206-7273

SYLVIA WEINSTOCK CAKES

THE QUEEN OF CAKES

273 CHURCH
STREET #3A
NEW YORK, NY
10013
212-925-6698

....

SYLVIA
WEINSTOCK.COM

Once you have seen Sylvia Weinstock's cakes, you will understand why she has been referred to variously as the Leonardo da Vinci of Cakes, the Queen of Wedding Cakes, and the Reigning Cake Diva. Originally a schoolteacher, Sylvia trained to be a pastry chef. Realizing she wanted to do something a little different and that no one was making custom, high-end wedding cakes, she set up her business in 1975 with a mission to create not only striking masterpieces, but also cake that tasted good. To that end, she uses only the crème de la crème of ingredients, and she never uses fondant—and the end product is something to remember. Her coterie of employees sit all day long, deftly crafting hundreds if not thousands of flowers out of sugar to adorn the cakes. Sylvia's business has grown by word of mouth, and she often feeds the rich and famous (as well as everyone else, too). Though tiny in stature (and always with her signature giant glasses adorning her face), Sylvia has a huge presence, and her cakes—which regularly require a construction crew and a team of engineers—often tower over her. Her biggest cake fed two thousand people; her highest cake stood twenty feet. Both Sylvia and her cakes are legendary and memorable.

TEA & SYMPATHY
AN ENGLISH RETREAT

Tea & Sympathy was started in the early 1990s by Nicky Perry as a café on Greenwich Avenue in the West Village that served traditional British fare, including sweet treats like treacle tart, sticky toffee pudding, spotted dick, and apple crumble (served with tea, of course). Later, she bought an adjacent storefront and turned it into a charming sweets shop. There you can grab Crunchies, Murray Mints, Mars Bars (the U.K. ones taste different—is it the cows?), Hob Nobs, Malteasers, Toffee Crisps, Cadbury's chocolates, and more. The British version of M&Ms, called Smarties, are well represented, and so are Devon Fudge, Dundee Cakes, and McVities Digestives in milk chocolate, dark chocolate, and plain. If you do not see what you are craving, perhaps one of the jolly folks behind the counter will help—their wicked sense of humor comes free of charge. It's all enough to bring tears to the eyes of homesick expats.

108 GREENWICH AVE.
NEW YORK, NY 10011
212-989-9735
············
TEAANDSYMPATHY
NEWYORK.COM

VOSGES HAUT-CHOCOLAT

A TREAT FOR EVERY MOOD

SoHo
132 SPRING STREET
NEW YORK, NY
10012
212-625-2929
....

Upper East Side
1100 MADISON AVE.
NEW YORK, NY
10028
212-717-2929
....

VOSGES
CHOCOLATE.COM

The founder of Vosges Haut-Chocolat, Katrina Markoff, trained in Paris at Le Cordon Bleu. After studying and traveling the world, Katrina returned to her native Chicago, where she experimented in her own kitchen. She proceeded to launch an artisanal chocolate empire, drawing inspiration not only from her travels but also from her need to create an imaginary world through chocolate. The combinations of nuts, spices, and flowers from places like Australia, Argentina, Venezuela, Budapest, and Mexico, induce thoughts of faraway places as they explode in your mouth. Luckily for me, there is a Vosges store near where I live, and I go there quite often. The dark oak shelves and glass vitrines are lined with all the amazing chocolate treats Katrina has created, making it feel like a library of chocolate. Vosges is a feast for the eyes as well as the taste buds and, ultimately, the soul. Whatever your mood, the array will not disappoint, whether you feel like chocolate mixed with bacon, blood oranges, black salt caramel, or peanut butter, to name but a few of the exotic selections. The staff is always smiling and ready to guide you through what Katrina describes as "storytelling through the medium of chocolate."

Strawberry Cocoa Nib Shortcake

FROM THE KITCHEN OF VOSGES HAUT-CHOCOLAT

FOR THE SHORTCAKE

- 1 CUP ALL-PURPOSE FLOUR
- ½ CUP WHOLE WHEAT PASTRY FLOUR
- 2 TEASPOONS BAKING POWDER
- 1½ TABLESPOONS SUGAR
- 1½ TEASPOONS SALT
- 4 TABLESPOONS COLD UNSALTED BUTTER, CUT INTO SMALL PIECES
- ⅔ CUP HEAVY CREAM, PLUS ADDITIONAL FOR BRUSHING
- 1 TABLESPOON TURBINADO SUGAR (SUCH AS SUGAR IN THE RAW)

FOR THE STRAWBERRY MUST

- 2 PINTS STRAWBERRIES, WASHED, HULLED, AND CUT IN HALF
- 1½ CUPS SUGAR
- 2 TABLESPOONS COCOA NIBS
- 1 TEASPOON ORANGE FLOWER WATER (OPTIONAL)

FOR THE MASCARPONE CREAM

- 8 OUNCES MASCARPONE CHEESE
- 2 TABLESPOONS VOLCANO ISLAND OR MANUKA HONEY
- ½ TEASPOON GRATED MEYER LEMON ZEST (YELLOW PART ONLY; NO WHITE)

FOR THE GARNISH (OPTIONAL)

- 1½ TABLESPOONS BALSAMIC VINEGAR

MAKE THE SHORTCAKE

1. Preheat the oven to 400°F. Line a baking sheet with parchment paper.

2. Whisk the flours, baking powder, sugar, and salt together. Cut the butter in with a fork or pastry blender until the butter is in small pea-sized pieces. Stir in the cream just until a dough forms. Gather the dough into a ball with your hands and gently knead together once or twice on a lightly floured surface. Roll or pat out the dough into a 6-inch square (at least ½ inch thick—be precise for a tall, lovely biscuit). Brush the dough with a bit of cream and sprinkle with turbinado sugar, then cut into 4 squares.

3. Place on the prepared baking sheet and bake on the center rack of the oven until golden, 17 to 20 minutes. Transfer the shortcakes to a wire rack to cool slightly. While the shortcakes are still slightly warm, split each in half horizontally with a serrated knife. Shortcakes can be made 2 days ahead of time and kept in an airtight container.

MAKE THE STRAWBERRY MUST:

1. Combine the strawberries, sugar, cocoa nibs, and orange flower water in a bowl, cover, and let macerate at room temperature for 1 hour to make a delicious strawberry juice. This can be made the morning of the event.

MAKE THE MASCARPONE CREAM

1. Combine the mascarpone, honey, and lemon zest. Cover and keep in the refrigerator until ready to serve. The mascarpone cream can be made the night before.

2. Plate the bottom half of the shortcake and put a generous spoonful of the strawberry must on the cake, followed by some of the strawberries and a drizzle of balsamic, if using. Top with a large dollop (about 2 tablespoons) of the mascarpone cream and follow with the top half of the shortcake. Serve immediately.

TIPS

A pastry blender utensil will help you cut the butter into the flour a bit easier than a fork. But both methods are fine.

Always confirm the temperature of the oven with a thermometer. Your oven may run hot or cold, and this could cause variation in recipe outcome. You can buy a decent oven thermometer at a hardware store for less than $10. You can make sure it is reading correctly (calibrate the thermometer) by hanging it on the edge inside of a pan with 1 inch of water at a full boil. Let the thermometer steam for a minute and then read it (without touching it—its hot!). It should read as 100°C or 212°F.

Finally, never use baking soda instead of baking powder or your shortcakes will be overly bitter and salty. I made the mistake by accident and boy was I sorry.

Sweets Sampler: Croissants

THE SECRET TO A GOOD CROISSANT IS IN THE DOUGH—the layer upon layer of butter and flour that make up puff pastry. Break open a croissant just out of the oven and it yields its secrets in a puff of steam – the melted butter having left behind an airy, flaky interior that melts in your mouth just as you delight in the crust of the outside.

PRETZEL CROISSANT

BIRDBATH // PG 17
The crunch of salt and sesame seeds on this croissant will transport you to another planet. Then you'll reach the light and flaky interior of this amazing confection and your rocket ship will really blast off.

CROISSANT

ALMONDINE BAKERY // PG 143
This is a classic croissant, perfectly executed. It's crisp and crunchy on the outside, buttery and airy on the inside with its thousands of layers of puff pastry.

ALMOND CROISSANT

CECI-CELA // PG 66
Great almond flavor in this croissant and the texture is just superb, from the almond cream to the glaze sprinkled with almonds and confectioners' sugar.

CHOCOLATE ALMOND CROISSANT

FRANCOIS PAYARD BAKERY // PG 39
This is a beautifully moist croissant with nice almond flavor, kicked into overdrive by the presence of chocolate and sprinkled with confectioners' sugar and chewy almonds.

MINI CHOCOLATE CROISSANT

BAKERI // PG 153
This is a classic *pain au chocolat* with deep, rich chocolate flavor. It's beautifully browned and crisp on the outside and comes in an adorable mini size.

ALMOND CROISSANT

BIEN CUIT // PG 156
Theirs has brandy added, which gives the almond flavor more depth. Moist and delicious, it's mildly sweet but wholly addictive.

New York
Sweets

EAST VILLAGE AND
LOWER EAST SIDE

BABYCAKES

A VEGAN REVELATION

Erin McKenna was diagnosed with wheat and dairy allergies in 2004. And thank heavens for that, since it was these allergies that inspired her to start Babycakes, a vegan bakery on Broome Street on the Lower East Side. The baked products are natural, organic, and free from common allergens (to the uninitiated: wheat, gluten, dairy, casein, and eggs). Erin chooses the sweeteners with care, and they are used sparingly. Very little white sugar or chemical sweeteners can be found in anything she bakes. Instead, most products are sweetened with agave nectar, a natural syrup that comes from cactuses and coconuts. You may be wondering what is left in the cakes to enjoy, but do not judge until you have tried her wonderful creations. Start with a cupcake (choose from vanilla, carrot, chocolate, and red velvet), then move on to the cakes: vanilla, chocolate, carrot, and lemon. Throw in a brownie or two and, should you need to convince yourself further that vegans are not missing out on anything, finish off with a loaf of banana chocolate chip bread or gingerbread, or maybe a big chocolate chip cookie. Whatever you do, definitely do not leave without trying the apple pie. At Babycakes, vegans can have their cake and eat it, too.

248 BROOME STREET
NEW YORK, NY
10002
212-677-5047
....
BABYCAKESNYC.COM

BLACK HOUND NEW YORK
A EUROPEAN PASTRY SHOP

170 2ND AVENUE
NEW YORK, NY
10003
212-979-9505
....
BLACKHOUNDNY.COM

In 1988, Black Hound opened in the East Village, and it is still going strong. Its loyal fans come for the handmade chocolates, cakes, cookies, pastries, and confections, and it is easy to see why the bakery is such a success: Just for a short time, patrons can leave New York City behind as they enter this little European pastry shop. The presentation alone will blow you away as you feast your eyes on pure perfection. Where to begin? Let temptation take over as you look at the cookies: raspberry sandwich hearts, ginger-lemon flowers, poppy seed daisies, lemon shortbread, and chocolate-orange oatmeal cookies, to mention but a few. If you need to sink your teeth into something more, there are cakes galore, from traditional carrot cake to chocolate cheesecake to flourless chocolate hazelnut cake. Black Hound's signature cake, the Busy Bee, will wow you with its three layers of chocolate cake, two layers of almond butter, and two layers of bittersweet chocolate mousse, all bathed in bittersweet chocolate. The award-winning assorted truffles are also not to be missed, and you'll be doing yourself a favor if you ask for a few almond petals and some chocolate-almond bark. But my very favorites are the miniature cake replicas, which look and taste just like the big ones but allow for more sampling. I like to buy at least six for a dinner party, and then slice and taste until there isn't a crumb left.

The miniature cake replicas, look and taste just like the big ones but allow for more sampling. Buy at least six for a dinner party.

It's hard to resist a box of boozy ganache bonbons infused with bourbon, tequila, elderflower liqueur, and other flavors.

BOND STREET CHOCOLATE

TOTEMS TO LIFT THE SPIRIT

Lynda Stern opened Bond Street Chocolate in 2009 in a petite store on the Lower East Side. Her spiritual side plays out in the chocolates she designs, including chocolate Buddhas coated with edible gold; figures of Ganesh, the elephant-headed Hindu deity; Jesus; and the Virgin of Guadalupe, among others. The individual chocolate pieces are beautifully displayed in a glass case, like gems in a jewelry store. It's hard to resist a box of boozy ganache bonbons infused with bourbon, tequila, elderflower liqueur, and other flavors. Chocolate skulls inspired by Keith Richards fill round silver boxes, and the milk chocolate bar with caramelized almonds and sea salt gives "candy bar" a new meaning. Just as I was looking around the dollhouse-size shop, mesmerized by the perfect chocolate statues, bonbons, and bars, Lynda brought out the *pièce de résistance* and gave it to me as a gift. Botticelli's "Birth of Venus" is one of my favorite paintings ever, and there it was, perfectly represented in chocolate. I was speechless! No guilt here: Religion is alive and well at Bond Street, in the shape of chocolate.

63 EAST 4TH
STREET
NEW YORK, NY
10003
212-677-5103
....

BONDST
CHOCOLATE.COM

CATHCART & REDDY

UPSCALE DESSERTS, A DOWNTOWN CROWD

6 CLINTON STREET
NEW YORK, NY
10002
212-228-0701
....
DESSERTTRUCK.COM

Formerly the DessertTruck, Cathcart & Reddy opened in 2011 on the Lower East Side. Jerome Chang, a co-owner and the executive chef, used to be a lawyer, but he gave up the law to make a different kind of dough. After going to the Culinary Institute of America and doing a stint in Le Cirque's pastry kitchen, Jerome wanted to make the finest of gourmet desserts, as seen on the menus of the city's most expensive restaurants, but accessible to all. The warm chocolate bread pudding and the warm molten chocolate cake are legendary. The vanilla crème brûlée is memorable, as are the brioche doughnut squares filled with Nutella. Yum! If you've never had *affogato*, ice cream drowned in espresso and topped with whipped cream, this is the one to try. The delicious hot chocolate actually somehow betters itself when made into frozen hot chocolate, and the great big chocolate chip cookies (and double chocolate chip ones, too!) do not disappoint. And let's not forget the *macarons*: salted caramel, passion fruit, or chocolate? Decisions, decisions. It is all happening at this charming dessert hot spot that stays open until 11 p.m. every night. Note that on the menu, desserts are listed under the heading "large desserts"—now *that* is my kind of dessert!

Chocolate Molten Cake

FROM THE KITCHEN OF CATHCART & REDDY

FOR THE OLIVE OIL GANACHE

1¾ OUNCES DARK
    CHOCOLATE (72%
    CACAO)

1¾ TEASPOONS OLIVE OIL

1   TEASPOON UNSALTED
    BUTTER

FOR THE CAKE

VEGETABLE OIL OR COOKING
    SPRAY FOR GREASING

2½ OUNCES UNSWEETENED
    CHOCOLATE

SCANT ½ CUP GRANULATED
    SUGAR

6   TABLESPOONS UNSALTED
    BUTTER

½   CUP BEATEN EGGS (2 TO
    3 LARGE)

1½ TEASPOONS
    ALL-PURPOSE FLOUR

PINCH OF SALT

TO SERVE

SEA SALT OR KOSHER SALT

ICE CREAM

WHIPPED CREAM

CANDIED NUTS, CRUSHED

1. Make the olive oil ganache: In a medium heatproof mixing bowl set over a saucepan filled with simmering water, put the chocolate, oil, and butter. Stir with a rubber spatula until the mixture is completely liquid and shiny. Carefully pour the ganache into four 1-ounce silicone molds or timbales. Place in the refrigerator to cool completely and set. The ganache can be made up to 3 days ahead and kept in the refrigerator.

2. Make the cakes: Preheat the oven to 300°F. Line four 10-ounce metal rings: Cut four strips of parchment paper a little longer than the circumference and a little wider than the height of the rings. Lightly oil the inside of each ring with oil. Line the inside of each ring with a parchment strip, then lightly oil the paper. Set the rings on a baking sheet.

3. Using the same double boiler setup used for the ganache, bring the water to a simmer. Put the chocolate, sugar, and butter in the same bowl used to make the ganache. Stir with a rubber spatula until the mixture is completely melted; it will remain grainy from the sugar. Take the bowl off the heat. Add the eggs, flour, and salt and continuously stir until the batter is uniform; this may take 1 to 2 minutes.

4. Fill a piping bag with the batter. Pipe each ring about half full. Place one ganache piece on top of the batter in each ring. Fill the rings about ½ inch from the top with the batter. Place the baking sheet with the rings in the oven and bake for 12 to 15 minutes, until the tops are just set.

5. Lift the rings off each cake using tongs. Gently peel the parchment off. Slide a small offset spatula underneath a cake and carefully transfer to a plate. To serve, sprinkle each warm cake with a pinch of salt, then top with a scoop of your favorite ice cream, whipped cream, and some nuts.

CECI-CELA
TASTE OF PARIS

55 SPRING STREET
NEW YORK, NY
10012
212-274-9179

CECICELANYC.COM

Ceci-Cela is a French patisserie *par excellence* nestled in a tiny shop on Spring Street in New York City but bursting with the flavors of France. Chef Laurent Dupal has presided over Ceci-Cela for fifteen-plus years. The entrance to the bakery is charming, and upon entering it is hard to imagine that you haven't stumbled into a patisserie in the middle of Paris. The essence of French pastry is the croissant, and you will not be disappointed with this version. It is flaky, light, and buttery, and the *pain au chocolat*, equally as flaky and buttery, is also bursting with dark chocolate. The almond croissant, my favorite, is filled with almond cream (frangipane) and bathed in sliced almonds. The Linzer tart butter cookies are layered with raspberry jam, and the *palmiers* are delectable baked swirls of caramelized puff pastry. If the cookies don't completely tickle your fancy, take home a lemon tart to make your cheeks pucker, a pear tart in an almond crust, or a tarte tatin with apples and pastry cream. For the chocolate lovers among you, the chocolate cake with genoise and chocolate ganache topped with truffles will give you a thrill not soon forgotten. It's better than a trip to Paris.

CLINTON ST. BAKING COMPANY

FEEL THE LOVE

Neil Kleinberg and DeDe Lahman opened Clinton St. Baking Company in April 2001, and love is in the air and in everything they do. They set out to make the best baked goods in New York City, using the freshest ingredients, and the lines started forming almost immediately. Locals and tourists from around the world come for the legendary blueberry pancakes which were voted by *New York* magazine as the best in New York City not once but twice. The fruit pies—apple, sour cherry, blueberry, and peach—in lattice crusts are sumptuous, moist, and fragrant. Try the extra-thick milk shake, a hernia for your tongue, and the hot fudge sundae, which is sure to rival the best you've ever had. Go with friends, get all the forks you need, then order the black-and-white layer cake, carrot cake, coconut lemon curd cake, or fresh strawberry layer cake. Move on to the cookies, brownies, and cupcakes . . . and, oh, those cream pies! Forget your diet, it is so worth it. All of the baked goods are made on premises from all-natural ingredients. Arrive at 8 a.m., just as the muffins and scones are coming out of the oven, and you'll see for yourself that there is nothing like them—except for everything else made at Clinton St. Baking. Don't be put off by the lines; it is worth the wait.

4 CLINTON STREET
NEW YORK, NY
10002
646-602-6263
....
CLINTONSTREET
BAKING.COM

Chocolate Banana Creme Pie

MAKES 12

FROM THE KITCHEN OF CLINTON ST. BAKING COMPANY

FOR THE CRUST

- 1¼ CUPS GRAHAM CRACKER CRUMBS
- ½ CUP (1 STICK) UNSALTED BUTTER, MELTED
- 1 TABLESPOON SUGAR
- ½ TEASPOON PURE VANILLA EXTRACT

FOR THE CHOCOLATE PUDDING

- 2 CUPS MILK
- 3 TABLESPOONS SUGAR
- 1½ TEASPOONS PURE VANILLA EXTRACT
- 1 LARGE EGG PLUS 2 LARGE EGG YOLKS
- ¼ CUP PLUS 2 TABLESPOONS UNSWEETENED COCOA POWDER
- 2 TABLESPOONS CORNSTARCH
- ¼ TEASPOON SALT
- 1 CUP SEMISWEET CHOCOLATE CHIPS
- 2 TABLESPOONS UNSALTED BUTTER

FOR THE WHIPPED CREAM

- 2¼ CUPS HEAVY CREAM
- 2 TEASPOONS PURE VANILLA EXTRACT
- 3 TABLESPOONS SUGAR

TO ASSEMBLE THE PIE

- 3 TO 4 BANANAS
- 6-OUNCE BLOCK DARK CHOCOLATE

MAKE THE CRUST

1. Preheat the oven to 350°F.

2. Stir all the ingredients together until the crumbs are moist. Pat into the bottom of a 9-inch pie plate. Bake for 10 to 12 minutes, until lightly browned. Set aside to cool completely.

MAKE THE CHOCOLATE PUDDING

1. In a saucepan, combine the milk, sugar, and vanilla and slowly bring to a boil.

2. Meanwhile, in a large bowl, combine the egg, egg yolks, cocoa powder, cornstarch, and salt. Melt the chocolate chips in a microwave oven, cooking for 30-second intervals until melted.

3. When the milk mixture is boiling, add a small amount of it to the egg and cocoa mixture. Mix in the remaining hot milk mixture, then return it all to the saucepan and continue to cook. When the pudding begins to thicken, add the melted chocolate. Continue to whisk especially to avoid the pudding burning on the bottom of the pan. Add the butter. The pudding is done when it thickens more and bubbles rise to the surface.

4. Pour into a bowl and put a sheet of plastic wrap directly on the surface of the pudding to prevent a skin from forming. Let cool completely.

MAKE THE WHIPPED CREAM

1. In a stand mixer with the whisk attachment, combine the cream and vanilla and beat on medium speed. Increase the speed as the cream starts to thicken. Whipping constantly, add the sugar. Whip until soft peaks form. Keep cold.

2. Into the baked and cooled crust, slice the bananas. Spread the chocolate pudding over the bananas. Spread the whipped cream over the pudding, making a mound in the middle to give the pie height.

3. Put the block of chocolate in the microwave and cook for 10 seconds. Using a vegetable peeler, peel the chocolate over the whipped cream to make chocolate curls.

4. Refrigerate for 10 to 20 minutes before serving to allow the pie to set. Store in the refrigerator for 3 to 4 days.

DESSERT CLUB, CHIKALICIOUS

BELLY UP TO THE BAR

204 EAST 10TH
STREET
NEW YORK, NY
10003
212-995-9511
....

DESSERT
CLUBNYC.COM

Imagine a restaurant that serves only desserts. Actually, there is no need to imagine such a place. Thanks to Chika and Don Tillman, it really exists, it's called Dessert Club, ChickaLicious, and it's located on Tenth Street in the East Village, where it's been serving innovative desserts since 2003. So original and sumptuous are the desserts that its patrons are prepared to queue up patiently for sixty minutes during peak periods. The twenty-seat dessert bar is for the passionate and serious dessert lover, and it is not just about savoring the delicacies. The kitchen is open, and visitors can watch the careful preparation and plating of all the dishes. The first time you visit, you may think you have found your favorite choice, but the menu changes daily, so your favorite choice will change every time you stop in. So vast is the selection that it feels as if you are traveling around the world in one sitting: fromage blanc island "cheesecake," mocha and hazelnut trifle with white coffee ice cream, honey parfait in five-citrus gazpacho with pistachio lace *tuile*, duo of apple baked in parchment paper with vanilla and caramel ice cream, lemongrass *panna cotta* with pineapple sorbet and poppy seed puff, warm chocolate tart with pink peppercorn ice cream and red wine sauce. My absolute favorite is the cookie éclair ice cream cone, filled with the best soft-serve vanilla I have ever tasted and topped with hot fudge.

FAY DA BAKERY

A CHINATOWN FIXTURE

After years of baking for other people, Han Chow decided to go it alone and opened his first bakery in 1991. Now, more than twenty years later, he has numerous bakeries around the city. Amid the hustle and bustle of Chinatown stands the Fay Da on the corner of Mott and Canal streets. Step in and join locals as well as out-of-towners who have come to one of the most trafficked corners in Chinatown to buy Chinese pastries, cookies, and buns. You won't find any fortune cookies or almond cookies here; instead, there are buns that are light, full of surprises, and not very sweet. Try buns like cream and coconut, chocolate chip walnut, and raisin and cheese. No true New York City bakery would be complete without cheesecake, and this spot is no exception. The bakery also turns out tempting mousses, sponge cakes, cookies, and tarts. Who needs fortune cookies when you have Fay Da?

Chinatown
83 MOTT STREET
NEW YORK, NY
10013
212-791-3884
....
191 CENTRE STREET
NEW YORK, NY
10013
212-966-8934
....
Queens
41-33 KISSENA BLVD.
FLUSHING, NY
11355
718-460-8018
....
7 ADDITIONAL
QUEENS LOCATIONS
SEE WEBSITE FOR
MORE INFO
....
FAYDA.COM

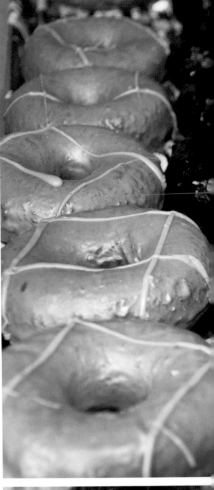

CHOC
OLATE ● YE

NUT
CREAM

ANILLA
BEAN ● YEAST
DOUGHNUT

DOUGH-NUT PLANT
NEW YORK CITY

CRYSTALLIZ
GINGER

CRÉM
BRÜL

ANILLA
EAN AND
JAM ● FILLED
DOUGHNUT

PEANUT
BUTTER
AND JAM

CRAN
BERRY ● YEAST
DOUGHNUT

ROASTED
CHES
TNUT

NN
ON
N ● YEAST
DOUGHNUT

DOUGHNUT PLANT
YORK CITY

DOUGHNUT PLANT
LOWER EAST SIDE LANDMARK

In 1994, in the basement of a tenement building on the Lower East Side, Mark Israel began his doughnut empire with his grandfather's father's recipe, which he found by chance in an old suitcase. When I first met Mark many years ago in his small bake shop, he walked me through the process of making the perfect handmade doughnut. Mark treated these doughnuts as if they were a life-saving elixir. I watched him make the dough, divide it to rest, and then, after a few hours, carefully drop the doughnuts, one by one, into a vat of hot oil. He turned them individually with chopsticks, as if playing a game. When they cooled, he either stuffed them or iced them, all by hand. Mark was a one-man doughnut operation. And, as the city was waking up every morning, Mark delivered his creations on his bicycle. In 2000, with the help of funds from his family, he opened the Doughnut Plant on Grand Street, and the word was out. Lines snaked out the door and sometimes down the block, and Mark was no longer an underground baker. In 2004, Mark invented the square jelly doughnut, so that while you're eating it you are also not wearing it. Since all of the doughnuts are made with fresh ingredients, many flavors are seasonal. The Valrhona chocolate is always on the menu, however, along with oatmeal, chocolate chip with pecans, salted peanut, crème brûlée, *tres leches*, strawberry, and coconut cream, among many others that will have your mouth watering. These are doughnuts like no other. Mark is a big guy with a big heart, and his doughnuts are a labor of love.

Lower East Side
379 GRAND STREET
NEW YORK, NY
10002
212-505-3700
············
Chelsea
220 WEST 23RD
STREET
(AT CHELSEA HOTEL)
NEW YORK, NY
10011
212-675-9100
············
DOUGHNUT
PLANT.COM

FERRARA BAKERY & CAFÉ

WONDERLAND OF ITALIAN SWEETS

195 GRAND STREET
NEW YORK, NY
10013
212-226-6150
....
FERRARACAFE.COM

In 1892, Antonio Ferrara opened his business on Grand Street on the Lower East Side so that he and his friends would have a place to go for an espresso and something sweet after the opera. Today, Ferrara is still in the same location, and still a family-owned business, run by the fifth generation of Ferraras and Lepores. In this pastry wonderland, it is hard to know where to begin, but for me, the miniature pastries are the prizes. The mini cannoli stuffed with thick cream made of ricotta cheese, chocolate chips, and candied fruit is so light that one is just not enough. The baby éclair is a one-bite marvel, and the Baba Rhum, stuffed with cream and soaked in rum, will make you swoon. My favorite is the mini *sfogliatella*, a paper-thin pastry shaped like a shell made with ricotta cheese, farina, and candied fruit. The Cassata cake, a soft sponge cake filled with ricotta, is considered the cornerstone of southern Italian desserts (and the deliciousness of this one would make any *nonna* jealous). The chocolate truffle cake, the Italian cheesecake, and the tiramisu will have you singing arias of praise. And just when you think you have perused the entire pastry cabinet and are ready to make a choice, you see the selection of gelati and sorbets! The coffee choices are so varied, a person could get a caffeine buzz just reading the menu. The Black Tie is my favorite: double espresso, black sambuca, and, of course, a big dollop of whipped cream on top. Ferrara is old-world Italian and, at this point, old-world New York.

BIG GAY ICE CREAM SHOP
A RAINBOW OF FLAVORS

Remember the days when the ice cream truck turned onto your street, rang its bells, and your Pavlovian response would kick in for a cone? Well, why live in the past when the present is so much better? Co-founders Douglas Quint and Bryan Petroff started the Big Gay Ice Cream Truck in 2009, and the mobile joint quickly became so successful that they then opened a brick-and-mortar shop in the East Village. The original flavors will bring a smile to your face, and the fun, good will, and sense of humor all come free of charge. My two favorites are the Salty Pimp (delicious soft-serve vanilla ice cream shot through with *dulce de leche* and finished off with sea salt and chocolate dip) and the American Globs (vanilla ice cream, pretzels, sea salt, and chocolate dip). But who I am to tell you what to choose? There is the Bea Arthur, a more simplistic confection featuring vanilla ice cream, *dulce de leche*, and crushed Nilla wafers. The adventurous should try the Cococone (vanilla ice cream and toasted curried coconut), while the more conservative may enjoy the Mermaid (vanilla ice cream, key lime curd, crushed graham crackers, and whipped cream).

BIGGAYICECREAM.COM
125 EAST 7TH STREET ~ NEW YORK, NY 10009 ~ 212-533-09333

IL LABORATORIO DEL GELATO
ARTISANAL ITALIAN ICE CREAM

Jon Snyder's love affair with ice cream began at an early age, at his grandparents' ice cream store in Westchester County, just north of New York City. So enamored was he that he went to Italy at age nineteen and discovered gelato. This opened a whole new world for him, and he started the Ciao Bella Gelato Co. in 1983, then sold it in 1989. This was only the beginning of Jon's ice cream career. He opened Il Laboratorio del Gelato in 2002 on Orchard Street, offering nearly two hundred flavors of gelato and sorbet. Enter and you will see a window to an open kitchen, where the ice cream is made in small batches. Although Jon travels the world for ingredients, he also likes to use local products, and when he puts a flavor on the menu, he *really* puts it on the menu: the apple sorbet comes in green, Fuji, Gala, Braeburn, and Honeycrisp versions. Grape comes in black, Concord, green, and red. You can make it easy on yourself and choose papaya, watermelon, or *yuzu* (at least there is only one type of these). Then there are the twelve different types of chocolate gelato. Jon is as sweet as the ice cream he makes, and his mother, who works there, will tell you the same.

LABORATORIODELGELATO.COM
188 LUDLOW STREET ~ NEW YORK, NY 10002 ~ 212-343-9922

VAN LEEUWEN ICE CREAM
ICE CREAM MADE WITH A CONSCIENCE

Pete Van Leeuwen, Ben Van Leeuwen, and Ben's wife Laura O'Neill began the business in 2008 as a food truck. The popularity of the company's artisanal ice cream exploded, and the trio now has several storefronts. The milk and cream, from pasture-raised cows on an upstate farm, are free of hormones and antibiotics. Each supplier is chosen with care and respect for the environment. As you might expect, the three most popular flavors are vanilla, chocolate, and strawberry, but you haven't tasted those flavors until you've tasted them as made by Van Leeuwen. The menu changes according to the season, but a dependable list of flavors includes hazelnut, ginger, mint chip, coffee, Earl Grey, and pistachio. The Van Leeuwens have added to the menu pastries baked fresh daily, including extraordinarily good muffins, biscotti, chocolate chip cookies, and Piedmont hazelnut brown butter cake.

WOOLY'S ICE
LIGHTER THAN AIR

Wooly's Ice was started by three cousins, Danny Che, David Sat, and Kenneth Sa. The trio took a trip to Taiwan and there experienced an eye-opening treat: shaved ice. When they returned to New York City, they noticed that there was a lack of good Taiwan- and Hawaii-style shaved ice, so they started experimenting with recipes and different flavors in the hope of opening their own business. In 2011, Wooly's went from an idea to reality when they christened the Wooly's Ice cart at the South Street Seaport. The flavors include original (*dulce de leche*), green tea, lactose-free strawberry, and mango, with toppings like fresh berries, sea salt *leche*, kiwis, and chopped brownies. The flavored shaved ice is certainly tasty, but the best part is that since the ingredients are fresh and fruity, it's a low-cal and low-fat treat. One of the smiling cousins will happily serve you up this summery confection, which Wooly's calls the "perfect refreshing healthy snack."

VANLEEUWENICECREAM.COM
EAST VILLAGE 48½ EAST 7TH STREET ∼ NY, NY 10003
BOERUM HILL 81 BERGEN STREET ∼ BROOKLYN, NY 11217 ∼ 347-763-2979
GREENPOINT 632 MANHATTAN AVENUE ∼ BROOKLYN, NY 11222 ∼ 718-701-1630

FACEBOOK.COM/WOOLYS
SOUTH STREET SEAPORT ∼ NEW YORK, NY 10013 ∼ 917-885-3919

Grapefruit with Campari Sorbet

MAKES ABOUT 2 PINTS

FROM THE KITCHEN OF IL LABORATORIO DEL GELATO

2 CUPS FRESHLY
  SQUEEZED GRAPEFRUIT
  JUICE

⅓ CUP SUGAR

2 TABLESPOONS CAMPARI

There are so many luscious flavors to choose from, but if you're looking for a sorbet that will send you into a frenzy, here it is. If you do not have an ice cream maker, this and the following recipe are worth buying one for.

1. Combine the grapefruit juice, sugar, Campari, and ¼ cup water. Freeze in an ice cream maker according to the manufacturer's directions.

Bitter Chocolate Gelato

MAKES ABOUT 2 TO 3 PINTS

FROM THE KITCHEN OF IL LABORATORIO DEL GELATO

1¼ CUPS SUGAR

2⅓ CUPS MILK

1 CUP UNSWEETENED
  COCOA POWDER (70%
  CACAO)

4 OUNCES BITTERSWEET
  CHOCOLATE

5 LARGE EGG YOLKS

1. In a heavy saucepan, cook ¼ cup of the sugar with 1 teaspoon water over medium heat until the sugar starts to melt. Stir until the sugar is melted and a deep brown color.

2. Remove from the heat and set the pan in a larger pan of ice water to stop the cooking. Let cool.

3. Add the milk to the pan and cook over medium heat, stirring, until the caramel is melted. Whisk in the cocoa powder and set aside.

4. In the top of a double boiler over simmering water, melt the chocolate, then set aside.

5. In a large bowl, beat the egg yolks together with the remaining 1 cup sugar until thick and pale yellow. Gradually stir in the milk mixture, then the melted chocolate.

6. Place over medium heat and cook for 5 minutes.

7. Pour through a sieve into a bowl, let cool to room temperature, then cover and chill in the refrigerator overnight.

8. Freeze in an ice cream maker according to the manufacturer's directions.

il laboratorio
del gelato
FRIGOPLAST
il laboratorio
del gelato
ICE CREAM AND SORBET

LA CHURRERIA

THE PLACE FOR CHURROS

284 MULBERRY
STREET
NEW YORK, NY 10012
212-219-0400
....

LACHURRERIA
NYC.COM

Fortunately for New Yorkers, our city is not only the home of the United Nations, it is the United Nations of food, La Churreria being the perfect example. In 2011, LoLo Manso opened this spot on Mulberry Street and brought Spain's churro to Nolita. Churros are fried dough sticks that have been lightly dusted with sugar, and La Churreria's are crisp, chewy, fluffy, and moist, even though they're dry to the touch. The odd, skinny shape looks more like breakfast from the movie *Alien* than a sweet, delectable, mouthwatering treat, but once you dip one in a cup of warm, melted chocolate, you'll want to eat another and another. The Churros Rellenos, which is a bigger version (more like a sausage), is stuffed with fillings: chocolate, cream, or *dulce de leche*. There are other *delicioso* sweets from Spain here as well, but the churro is the star, and it's an extremely addictive once at that! The staff is friendly and very informative. Take yourself on a trip to Spain via this Nolita restaurant.

LIQUITERIA
FRESH-SQUEEZED SWEETS

If you are in need of an Afternoon D'Lite, a Reggae Rhumba, or a Tropical Kiss, Liquiteria is the place for you. This smoothie purveyor is a rock star in the world of juice bars. The freshly squeezed juices range from apple to wheat grass and everything in between, including grapefruit, orange, pear, pineapple, carrot, and watermelon. (Personally, I go for the watermelon-pineapple.) All can be spiked with ginger or the shop's famous Hot Shot: lemon, ginger, and cayenne. Doug Green is the father of the modern juice experience, and he brought raw, cold-juice pressing to New York City well before the cleanse and bottled-juice movements began. Doug was not only born with the name Green, but he also appropriately appreciates the benefits of living green through plant-based foods. With healthy, cleansing thoughts in mind and his mother's collection of juicing books from the 1950s and '60s in his hands, he created this juicing paradise. Cleanse your tired intestines at Liquiteria, which has been referred to as an urban oasis in a city that never stops. But stop you should, and it's almost a guarantee that you'll stop again and again.

170 2ND AVENUE
NEW YORK, NY
10003
212-358-0300
....
LIQUITERIA.COM

Golden Vanilla
with
Vanilla buttercream

Mott Street Cupcakes

A very sweet way to end an evening or start the day.

German Chocolate Cake

Lemon
a
bun

Marbled pound cake

Blue Velvet Cake

LITTLE CUPCAKE BAKESHOP

BROOKLYN-BASED TREATS

Little Cupcake Bakeshop is a family affair. Massimo LoBuglio and his brothers run the original shop in Bay Ridge, Brooklyn, and in 2010 they opened an outpost in the Nolita neighborhood. The crowds immediately lined up on Prince Street to sample its treats. As soon as you enter, the colors captivate your senses and the homey atmosphere makes you want to sit and stay a spell. Between the cakes on the countertop and the cupcakes below it, a whirlwind of colors and flavors toy with your ability to make an immediate and singular choice. The cakes (Chocolate Cloud, Luscious Lemon, Dreaming Princess, and Oreo, among others) are fluffy and light, and the cupcakes (vanilla, devil's food, red velvet, carrot, peanut butter, German chocolate, and strawberry, among others) are beyond expectation. Fresh fruit pies and brownie bars enjoy space alongside the gluten-free rice pudding (without question one of the creamiest I have ever eaten) and other pudding varieties. Massimo and his family are extremely civic-minded and donate to many environmental projects. The bakery is green through and through, and its products are organic. And since it's open late, it feels like an everyday treat to go by after dinner for a cup of coffee and a cupcake, a slice of cake, or a cup of pudding. Little Cupcake is a very sweet way to end an evening or start the day.

Nolita
30 PRINCE STREET
NEW YORK, NY
10012
212-941-9100
....

Brooklyn
9102 THIRD AVE.
BROOKLYN, NY
11209
718-680-4465
....

LITTLECUPCAKE
BAKESHOP.COM

Rice Pudding

FROM THE KITCHEN OF LITTLE CUPCAKE BAKESHOP

¾ CUP ARBORIO RICE

½ TEASPOON KOSHER SALT

5 CUPS HALF-AND-HALF

¾ CUP SUGAR

I LARGE EGG, BEATEN

I½ TEASPOONS PURE
    MADAGASCAR VANILLA
    BEAN PASTE

I TEASPOON GRATED
   ORANGE ZEST

We serve our rice pudding chilled, but it is just as delicious warm. This is a great recipe to get creative with: Add cinnamon, dried or fresh fruit, coffee, cocoa powder, or whatever strikes you—the possibilities are endless.

1. Combine the rice and salt with 1½ cups water in a medium heavy-bottomed stainless-steel saucepan. Bring to a boil, stir once, then lower the heat to very low and simmer, covered, for 8 to 9 minutes, until most of the water is absorbed.

2. Stir in 4 cups of the half-and-half and the sugar and bring to a boil. Simmer, uncovered, for 25 minutes, stirring often, especially toward the end, until the rice is very soft. Gradually stir in the egg and continue to cook for 1 minute. Remove from the heat and add the remaining 1 cup half-and-half, the vanilla bean paste, and orange zest. Stir well. Serve warm or chilled: If chilling, pour into a bowl and place a piece of plastic wrap directly on top of the pudding to prevent a skin from forming, then put in the refrigerator until very cold.

Strawberry Cupcakes

FROM THE KITCHEN OF LITTLE CUPCAKE BAKESHOP

FOR THE CUPCAKES

- 1 CUP (2 STICKS) UNSALTED BUTTER, SOFTENED
- 2 CUPS SUGAR
- 3 LARGE EGGS
- 1 TEASPOON PURE VANILLA EXTRACT
- 1 TEASPOON BAKING SODA
- ½ TEASPOON BAKING POWDER
- 3½ CUPS ALL-PURPOSE FLOUR
- ½ TEASPOON SALT
- 2 CUPS FINELY DICED STRAWBERRIES

FOR THE FROSTING

- 3 TABLESPOONS UNSALTED BUTTER, SOFTENED
- 2¼ CUPS CONFECTIONERS' SUGAR
- ¾ TEASPOON PURE VANILLA EXTRACT
- 2 TABLESPOONS WHOLE MILK

MAKE THE CUPCAKES

1. Preheat the oven to 350°F. Line cupcake tins with paper liners.

2. In a large bowl, using an electric mixer fitted with the paddle attachment, cream the butter and sugar until fluffy. Add the eggs one at a time, beating well after each addition, then beat in the vanilla, baking soda, baking powder, flour, and salt. Beat at high speed for 2 to 3 minutes, until combined.

3. Stir in the strawberries.

4. Spoon the batter into the cupcake tins, filling each two-thirds full. Bake for 20 minutes, or until a toothpick inserted in the center of a cupcake comes out clean. Remove to wire racks and let cool completely before icing.

MAKE THE FROSTING

1. In a large bowl, using an electric mixer fitted with the paddle attachment, beat the butter at high speed until fluffy.

2. Gradually add the confectioners' sugar, beating until smooth. Add the vanilla and milk and beat well. Using a knife, spread the frosting on the cooled cupcakes.

blueberry &
cream cookie

cornflake-marshmallow
chocolate chip cookie

DON'T MISS:
Crack Pie, Cereal Milk
Soft Serve, and
Compost Cookies

COFFEE
we proudly serve
STUMPTOWN espresso

ESPRESSO 2
CAPPUCINO 3.65
MACCHIATO 2.25
AMERICANO 3/3.50
LATTE 3.85
HOT CHOCOLATE 4
add marshmallows .50

Fancy ♥ SHAKES
contain alcohol
→ must be enjoyed inside store!

cereal milk white russian 9
(cereal milk, kahlua, vodka)

birthday shake
(b.day truffles, rum, cereal milk)

espresso *
(espresso, cereal milk, frangelico)

banana split mudslide *
(banana split, kahlua, vodka)

chocolate-covered pretzel
(cereal milk, pretzel milk, rum, fudge)

...RVE
...e cream 4.50
...al milk™
...ana split*

...nflake crunch .75
...opping

...AKES 6
... milk™
...l split*
...l milk
...so shake 7
...real milk ss, espresso)

...R +DRINKS
...ap pale ale 2.50
...nder stout 2.50

peanut butter cookie*

corn cookie

co

MOMOFUKU MILK BAR

PURVEYOR OF ADDICTIVE SWEETS

Started in 2008 and headed by award-winning pastry chef and owner Christina Tosi, this chain of sweet spots has nothing less than a cult following. Its five locations throughout New York City are all small, charming, and basic with an oversize blackboard listing the baked goods. These include the infamous Crack Pie—made of a toasted-oat crust and a gooey butter, sugar, and cream filling—which is as addictive as the drug it's named after. Also on offer are the delicious Blondie Pie, made with cashew brittle, and the Candy Bar Pie, which has a chocolate crust and a filling made of caramel, peanut butter nougat, and pretzels. The Compost Cookie (made of pretzels, potato chips, coffee, oats, butterscotch, and chocolate chips) and the Cornflake Cookie (cornflakes, marshmallows, and chocolate chips) are the stuff of legend. The soft-serve ice cream is light and creamy, and it comes in outrageous but delicious flavors like Cereal Milk, Blueberry Miso, and Guava Horchata. If it's cake you desire, grab a slice of the Apple Pie Cake (with cheesecake filling, apple compote, and pie crumbs) or the Chocolate Malt Cake (with malted milk crumbs and charred marshmallows). Both will have your taste buds in a frenzy. The Birthday Cake is a rainbow cake with layers of cake, cake crumbles, and vanilla frosting, but you don't need to wait for the big day (or the big cake—try it as a Cake Truffle, too!) to buy one. And if there's a wedding in your future, the shop offers one-, two-, three-, and four-tier varieties of its signature unique cakes for your special day. Momofuku Milk Bar is a dessert world unto its own, and Christina Tosi is the pied piper of sweet imagination.

East Village
251 EAST 13TH STREET
NEW YORK, NY
212-254-3500

Midtown
15 WEST 56TH STREET
NEW YORK, NY
10019
212-757-5878

Upper West Side
561 COLUMBUS AVE.
NEW YORK, NY
10024
347-577-9504

Williamsburg
382 METROPOLITAN AVENUE
BROOKLYN, NY
11211
347-577-9504

Carroll Gardens
360 SMITH STREET
BROOKLYN, NY
11231
347-577-9504

MILKBARSTORE.COM

Crack Pie

FROM THE KITCHEN OF MOMOFUKU MILK BAR

FOR THE OAT COOKIE

- ½ CUP (1 STICK) UNSALTED BUTTER, AT ROOM TEMPERATURE
- ⅓ CUP FIRMLY PACKED LIGHT BROWN SUGAR
- 3 TABLESPOONS GRANULATED SUGAR
- 1 LARGE EGG YOLK
- ½ CUP ALL-PURPOSE FLOUR
- 1½ CUPS OLD-FASHIONED ROLLED OATS
- ⅛ TEASPOON BAKING POWDER
- PINCH OF BAKING SODA
- ½ TEASPOON KOSHER SALT

FOR THE OAT COOKIE CRUST

- 1 TABLESPOON FIRMLY PACKED LIGHT BROWN SUGAR
- ¼ TEASPOON KOSHER SALT
- ABOUT 4 TABLESPOONS UNSALTED BUTTER, MELTED

MAKE THE OAT COOKIE

1. Preheat the oven to 350°F. Spray a quarter sheet pan or baking sheet with cooking spray (Pam) and line it with parchment, or just line the pan with a silicone baking mat.

2. In the bowl of a stand mixer fitted with the paddle attachment, cream the butter and sugars on medium-high speed for 2 to 3 minutes, until fluffy and pale yellow. Scrape down the sides of the bowl with a spatula. With the mixer on low speed, add the egg yolk, then increase the speed to medium-high and beat for 1 to 2 minutes, until the sugar granules are completely dissolved and the mixture is pale white.

3. With the mixer on low speed, add the flour, oats, baking powder, baking soda, and salt.

4. Mix for 1 minute, until the dough comes together and any remnants of dry ingredients have been incorporated. The dough will be a slightly fluffy, fatty mixture in comparison to your average cookie dough. Scrape down the sides of the bowl.

5. Plop the cookie dough in the center of the prepared pan and, with a spatula, spread it out until it is ¼ inch thick. The dough won't end up covering the entire pan; this is okay. Bake for 15 minutes, or until the cookie is caramelized on top and puffed slightly but set firmly. Let cool completely before proceeding. The cookie can be made up to 1 week ahead, wrapped well in plastic and refrigerated.

MAKE THE OAT COOKIE CRUST

1. Put the broken up oat cookie, brown sugar, and salt in a food processor and pulse it on and off until the cookie is broken down and has the consistency of wet sand.

2. Transfer the mixture to a bowl, add the butter, and knead until moist enough to form into a ball. If it is not moist enough to do so, melt an additional 1 to 1½ tablespoons butter and knead it in.

3. Divide the dough evenly between two 10-inch pie pans. Using your fingers and the palms of your hands, press the dough firmly into each pie pan, making sure the bottom and sides of the pan are evenly covered. Use the pie shells immediately, or wrap well in plastic and store at room temperature for up to 5 days or in the fridge for up to 2 weeks.

FOR THE FILLING

1½ CUPS GRANULATED
SUGAR

¾ CUP FIRMLY PACKED
LIGHT BROWN SUGAR

¼ CUP DRY MILK POWDER

¼ CUP CORN POWDER

1½ TEASPOONS KOSHER
SALT

1 CUP (2 STICKS)
UNSALTED BUTTER,
MELTED

¾ CUP HEAVY CREAM

½ TEASPOON PURE
VANILLA EXTRACT

8 LARGE EGG YOLKS

TO SERVE

CONFECTIONERS' SUGAR

MAKE THE FILLING

1. Put the sugars, dry milk powder, corn powder, and salt in the bowl of a stand mixer fitted with the paddle attachment and mix on low speed until thoroughly combined. Add the butter and beat for 2 to 3 minutes, until all the dry ingredients are moist. Add the cream and vanilla and continue mixing on low speed for 2 to 3 minutes, until any white streaks from the cream have completely disappeared into the mixture.

2. Scrape down the sides of the bowl with a spatula.

3. Add the egg yolks, beating them into the mixture on low speed just to combine; be careful to not aerate the mixture, but mix until it is glossy and homogenous. Use the filling right away or store in an airtight container in the refrigerator for up to 1 week.

4. When ready to bake, preheat the oven to 350°F.

5. Put both pie shells on a baking sheet. Divide the filling evenly between the crusts; the filling should fill them three quarters of the way full. Bake for 15 minutes. The pies should be golden brown on top but will still be very jiggly. Open the oven door and lower the oven temperature to 325°F. Depending on your oven it may take 5 minutes or longer for the oven to cool to the new temperature. Keep the pies in the oven during this process.

6. When the oven reaches 325°F, close the door and bake the pies for 5 minutes longer. The pies should still be jiggly in the bull's-eye center but not around the outer edges. If the filling is still too jiggly, leave the pie in the oven for an additional 5 minutes or so.

7. Gently take the pan of crack pies out of the oven and transfer to a wire rack to cool to room temperature. Freeze the pies for at least 3 hours, or overnight, to condense the filling for a dense final product—freezing is the signature technique, and the result is a perfectly executed crack pie. If not serving the pies right away, cover tightly in plastic wrap.

8. In the refrigerator they will keep for 5 days; in the freezer they will keep for 1 month.

9. Transfer the pies from the freezer to the refrigerator to defrost for at least 1 hour before you're ready to slice it. Serve your crack pie cold! Decorate with confectioners' sugar, either sifting it through a fine sieve or dispatching pinches with your fingers.

With nine pudding choices and fifteen toppings, there are more than thirty thousand possible pudding combinations!

PUDDIN'
CUSTOMER-CONSTRUCTED CREATIONS

102 ST. MARKS
PLACE
NEW YORK, NY
10009
212-477-3537
....

PUDDINNYC.COM

Puddin', on St. Marks Place in the East Village, opened in January 2012 and promptly sold out its entire stock in an hour and a half. The next day, it sold out in forty minutes. So what does Puddin' have that makes it special? Well, pudding. Customers construct their own creations, choosing among freshly made chocolate, vanilla, banana, butterscotch, coffee, lemon, coconut, and rice puddings. They then select toppings (there are nineteen available, including salted caramel sauce, maple-toasted granola, dried cherry compote, graham cracker crumbs, and red velvet cake). If you're too overwhelmed to make decisions, choose one of chef-owner Clio Goodman's signature puddings. The Classic has chocolate and butterscotch puddings with layers of whipped cream, and the Lemon Drop has tart lemon pudding with delicious crushed ginger crunch cookies and toasted marshmallow cream. The puddings come in three sizes: mini so you can have many, medium so you can enjoy your favorite, and large so you can indulge your inner pudding monster. The shop also sells freshly baked cookies, cakes, pies, and brownies. Bravo to these imaginative dessert creations!

Vanilla Pudding

FROM THE KITCHEN OF PUDDIN'

½ VANILLA BEAN

1¼ CUPS HEAVY CREAM

1¼ CUPS MILK

½ CUP SUGAR

⅛ TEASPOON SALT

3 TABLESPOONS CORNSTARCH

3 EGG YOLKS

1 TEASPOON VANILLA EXTRACT

1. Split the vanilla bean and scrape out the seeds.

2. In a small saucepan add the heavy cream, milk, and the vanilla bean and seeds. Cook over medium heat until the milk is hot and steamy.

3. Remove from the heat and cool to room temperature in the saucepan, about an hour.

4. To the cooled milk mixture, add the sugar, salt, cornstarch, and egg yolks and whisk until fully combined.

5. Place the saucepan over medium heat and whisk the mixture constantly until it starts to get thick and the whisk leaves an impression in the custard when lifted from the pot.

6. Strain immediately into a large bowl and stir in the vanilla extract. Cool for 10 minutes, then chill in the refrigerator for 1 to 2 hours, pressing a sheet of plastic wrap onto the surface of the pudding to prevent a skin from forming. Spoon up and serve.

Sweets Sampler: Brownies

AMERICANS ARE CRAZY ABOUT BROWNIES. Chewy and chocolatey, they are a common dessert—but all brownies are not created equal. At worst they are dry and have a one-note flavor. At best, they are a rich and decadent treat.

SWEET AND SALTY BROWNIE

BAKED // PG 148

This chocolatey, fudgy brownie has a perfect crackly top. It also has a layer of salted caramel in the center, and is sprinkled with coarse sugar and salt. If you like the salty-sweet combination, this is the brownie for you.

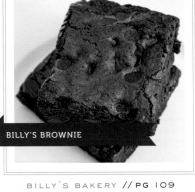

BILLY'S BROWNIE

BILLY'S BAKERY // PG 109

This is a chewy brownie, with a more cakelike texture, studded with little chocolate chips.

CHOCOLATE BROWNIE

MILK & COOKIES BAKERY // PG 31

Chewy and dense, this version has a rich and deep chocolate flavor. It is sprinkled with small chocolate chips. This is a chocolately wham! of a brownie.

BUTTERSCOTCH BROWNIE

CATHCART & REDDY // PG 62

This bar amazes with its maple/butterscotch flavor and deeply moist and cakelike texture. It's visually stunning too—with a beautiful swirl in texture on top.

COCONUT DREAM BAR

AMY'S BREAD // PG 14

A gooey bar with coconut and chocolate chips and a graham cracker crust. The flavors are balanced perfectly: just enough coconut, just enough chocolate, and just enough crust to hold it all together.

RASPBERRY BROWNIE

BAKERI // PG 153

There's something about the combination of dark dense chocolate and bright raspberry flavor that brings each ingredient to greater heights. The raspberries lighten the chocolate in the brownie and make it sing.

RICE TO RICHES

SWEET, CREAMY GRAINS OF LOVE

Rice to Riches is devoted entirely to rice pudding, and it does this dessert comfort food proud. The mod-looking outpost, located in the Nolita neighborhood, has twenty-plus flavors on offer. Its interior makes you feel like you've just entered the cafeteria of a spaceship, and the friendly staff is happy to make suggestions and let you try just about every flavor in the place before you decide. The atmosphere is alive with communal tasting and sharing, and you can hear sighs of "Oh, my," "Wow," and "This is outrageous." The Old Fashioned Romance is for purists, but if you are adventuresome, try the Coconut Coma, the Fluent in French Toast, the Almond Shmalmond, the Sex Drugs and Rocky Road, or the Chocolate Chip Flirt. There's also a roster of flavors that changes with the seasons, including the It Takes Two to Peach Mango, the Promise Me Passion Fruit, and the Milk Chocolate Only Rings Twice. Any rice pudding can be topped with the shop's inventive add-ons, which include oatmeal coconut crumble, toasted pound cake, buttery graham crackers, and even homemade raspberry jelly. Rice pudding aficionados will be bowled over at the selection, not to mention the texture and creaminess of the product.

37 SPRING STREET
NEW YORK, NY
10012
212-274-0008
....
RICETORICHES.COM

RUSS & DAUGHTERS

A CENTURY WORTH OF CHARM

179 EAST HOUSTON
STREET
NEW YORK, NY
10002
212-475-4880
············
RUSSAND
DAUGHTERS.COM

Joel Russ opened this smoked-fish emporium in 1914 on the Lower East Side. In 1920, he moved it to the location on Houston Street that is still its home today, and in 1933, when it became clear that he would pass on the business to his three daughters (unusual for the times, but he had no sons), he dubbed it Russ & Daughters. Four generations later, the store that's famous for its "appetizing" (per the company, "the foods one eats with bagels," meaning a variety of smoked and cured salmons, as well as cream cheese and other dairy—not "deli," per Jewish dietary laws) has some of the city's best Nova Scotia lox, whitefish, herring, sable, and sturgeon. For me, the custom-made sweets are what put Russ & Daughters over the top. The white porcelain vitrines that hold all the cakes, candy, and puddings are joined by big jars of mixed fruits, nuts, and halvah, an age-old confection of crushed sesame seeds, honey, and other indulgent ingredients such as chocolate, pistachios, or almonds. The store's macaroons and fresh-baked rugelach (a flaky buttery dough wrapped around a filling that can be either chocolate, raspberry, marmalade, or cinnamon and walnuts) are hard to beat, but for popularity I would say the apple strudel ranks right up there too: juicy apples, raisins, brown sugar, and cinnamon wrapped in a flaky blanket of dough. The dried fruits are plump and juicy, but it's the creamy, moist bagel pudding (which goes back all those four generations), made of big chunks of bagel, raisins, and prunes, that will really please your palate. The array of chocolates jogs childhood memories of putting jelly rings on my fingers and freezing (and then breaking into a hundred pieces) the marshmallow twist. Take a trip to Russ & Daughters—the sweets and the nostalgia will have you visiting again and again.

The sweets and the nostalgia will have you visiting again and again.

MEDJOOL DATES
8 99 LB

TURKISH FIGS
6 49 lb

Ambrosia
6.99 lb

RUSS & DAUGHTERS
Almond Covered
Halvah Bars
$1.99 each + tax

ECONOMY CANDY
SWEETS BY THE POUND

When Jerry Cohen's father opened Economy Candy in 1937, it was a typical corner candy store of its day. Bulk bins full of colorful hard candies enticed youngsters with their panorama of choices. Guys could buy their dolls a heart-shaped box of chocolates for Valentine's Day, fake wax lips for Halloween, specialty candy for Christmas, and so on. Barrels in the back room presented a geography lesson of nuts from around the world. Economy Candy is now a third-generation sweet tooth metropolis run by Jerry, his wife, and his son Mitchell. When I was little, I loved multicolored sugar buttons on reams of paper, Bonomo Turkish taffy in three flavors (which we froze and broke into a million pieces), gooey taffy in the shape of a peanut, Baby Ruth bars, Planters Peanut Bars, Red Hots, and nonpareils with little white balls that got stuck in my teeth. All of these back-in-the-day candies are still present at Economy Candy to remind me of my childhood. The nostalgia is overwhelming, but the past aside, the store sells every candy imaginable and then some, and its customers can buy a quarter-pound or fifty pounds of their favorite. Economy gives new meaning to the phrase "kid in a candy store."

ECONOMYCANDY.COM
108 RIVINGTON STREET ~ NEW YORK, NY 10002 ~ 212-254-1531

PAPABUBBLE
A DESIGNER CANDY SHOP

This unpretentious little candy store is easy to miss, and missing out on this experience would be a mistake. The owners, Fiona Ryan and Chris Grassi, hold candy workshops so Papabubble's customers can watch the entire process, from cooking to coloring to flavoring to shaping (to eating!). Sure, you can enter the store, make a purchase, and then leave, but you miss out if you do not wait for the performance (which occurs every few hours and takes about an hour an a half). Opened in 2007, the store is a mixture of a laboratory and a kitchen, with glass shelves containing rows of flasks, containers, and utensils. Opposite are inviting jars of eye-catching candy. There are lollipops and candies in flavors like cinnamon, strawberry, licorice, mint, anise, and lime, all in amusing shapes like bears, rings, toothbrushes, knots, tigers, glasses, bunnies, and even a set of dentures. My favorite is the licorice pillows, but if you want to try everything, get a bag of Morris Mix. The I Love New York mix is also dandy: each candy features the name of one of the five boroughs.

PAPABUBBLE.COM
380 BROOME STREET ~ NEW YORK, NY 10013 ~ 212-966-2599

THE SWEET LIFE
CHOCOLATE AND CANDY GALORE

Siblings Sam Greenfield and Diane Miller bought this neighborhood store in 2004 and stocked it to capacity with as many salty and sweet things they could find. This candy land is at the corner of Hester and Ludlow streets on the Lower East Side. The store's motto is "Anything can be dipped in chocolate," and the assortment is mind-boggling. The chocolate-dipped marshmallows rolled in M&Ms are a big hit, but if that doesn't strike your fancy, you can try chocolate-dipped apricots, oranges, caramel apples, raisins, and nuts, among other treats. The center of the store is a smorgasbord of dried fruits and nuts, just begging you to take a taste. Big, open bowls of cashew nuts from India sit next to pistachios, macadamia nuts from Hawaii, and trail mix. From fudge to halvah to jelly beans, Sam manages to find the biggest and freshest examples of everything, sourced from all around the world. If its licorice you seek, there are about twenty-five choices, but my favorite sweet here is the milk chocolate Oreo bark. The Sweet Life is a sweetheart of a candy store.

SIGMUND'S PRETZELS
HANDMADE YEASTY TWISTS

Sigmund's Pretzels, in the East Village, seems like it should be in the middle of Eastern Europe. The place is charming, and the pretzels are the best I've ever tasted. Although there are satellite choices, including jam-filled doughnuts, rum-raisin muffins, and huge cookies filled with peanut butter, chocolate chips, or pretzels (called Wanckos and named after the manager), there is no mistaking the star around which the others rotate: the pretzel. Lina Kulchinsky, a lawyer-turned–pastry chef, worked at Bouley Bakery and Jean Georges before opening the only artisanal pretzel shop of its kind in New York City. This delicious soft pretzel is crisp yet chewy on the outside and soft and moist on the inside. The cinnamon raisin is my absolute favorite, and although definitely not needed, you can opt for dips such as butter, cream cheese, jam, or Nutella. Bonus: If you're near the Metropolitan Museum of Art, Sigmund's operates a pretzel cart there, though this one is far, far beyond the typical New York City pretzel-cart orbit.

SWEETLIFENY.COM
63 HESTER STREET ∼ NEW YORK, NY 10002 ∼ 212-598-0092

SIGMUNDNYC.COM
29 AVENUE B ∼ NEW YORK, NY 10009 ∼ 646-410-0333
METROPOLITAN MUSEUM 82ND STREET AND FIFTH AVENUE ∼ NEW YORK, NY

TU-LU'S GLUTEN-FREE BAKERY

DELICIOUS TREATS WITHOUT WHEAT

338 EAST 11TH
STREET
NEW YORK, NY
10003
212-777-2227

TU-LUSBAKERY.COM

In 2009, Tully Lewis and Jen Wells, friends who united around a gluten-free lifestyle, opened their bakery in the East Village. Together they have created everything those on a gluten-free diet could wish for, including muffins, cookies, brownies, doughnuts, and coffee cakes. Their goods are not only gluten-free, but some are also dairy-free and suitable for vegans. But you don't have to be allergic to gluten to enjoy—Tully and Jen have come up with an endless variety of goodies to suit all tastes. Even the all-time favorite red velvet cake is available (either gluten-free or dairy-free), along with vanilla, chocolate, and spice cakes, all with a selection of fifteen different icing flavors. Try a blueberry muffin, a raspberry-almond crumble muffin, an individual coffee cake, or the Morning Glory muffin. There are dark chocolate brownies, peanut butter toffee blondies, vegan agave brownies, and agave cinnamon granola with almonds and cranberries. Everything is preservative-free and baked fresh daily on the premises. The shop even offers cakes for your gluten-free, dairy-free, or vegan wedding.

Rainbow Snowballs

FROM THE KITCHEN OF ZUCKER BAKERY

7   OUNCES TEA BISCUITS (PREFERABLY GOYA MARIA BRAND)

7   TABLESPOONS UNSALTED BUTTER

¼   CUP SUGAR

¼   CUP COCOA POWDER

½   CUP MILK

1   TEASPOON INSTANT ESPRESSO POWDER

1   CUP RAINBOW SPRINKLES

1. Grind the biscuits in a food processor and put them into a large bowl.

2. In a medium saucepan over low heat, melt the butter. Add in the sugar, cocoa powder, and milk, and stir until dissolved. Stir in the espresso powder. Pour this mixture over the ground biscuits.

3. Refrigerate the mixture until it is cold to the touch. Then, using your hands, shape the mixture into balls. Roll the balls in the sprinkles to coat.

4. Enjoy cold or at room temperature.

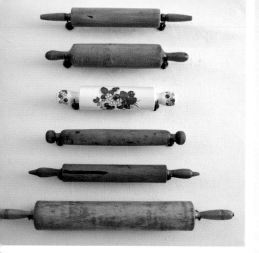

ZUCKER BAKERY

SWEETS WITH AN EXOTIC FLAIR

With a culinary background at Daniel and Bouley Bakery and inspiration from her family and friends, Zohar Zohar opened Zucker Bakery in the East Village in 2011. Her creations have an Israeli, European, and Moroccan flair, and her homemade treats are very special, starting with the best-selling Roses. These sweets are sometimes known as sticky buns or cinnamon rolls. The recipe at Zucker Bakery, however, belongs to Zohar's mother-in-law, and she calls them "Shoshanim," from the Hebrew word for "roses." Other options include the Honey Almond Fingers, which are so light and crumbly that you cannot stop at one. Or try the Play Date, made of a very thin layer of dough spiced with cinnamon and cloves. There are thin cookies made with dried fruit and nuts called the Love Loaf, just like Zohar's mother used to make. The light, tasty rugelach is Zohar's own version, with dates, almonds, and cloves, and her chocolate babka is a masterpiece. The lemon bars are tangy and fresh, but my favorite is the Alfajhores, a *dulce de leche*–filled cookie sandwich rolled in coconut flakes. It's such a thing of beauty that it's almost impossible to describe in words. Zohar's tried-and-true family recipes will warm your heart and tantalize your taste buds. The place is charming and quiet, so stay a while with a great cup of coffee and a piece of Love Loaf.

433 EAST 9TH
STREET
NEW YORK, NY
10009
646-559-8425
. . . .
ZUCKERBAKERY.COM

Sweets Sampler: Cupcakes

THE CUPCAKE CRAZE IS STILL GOING STRONG IN NEW YORK, though other contenders have arisen (cake pops! pie!). Bakeries have gotten ever more inventive in their cupcake offering—in size, appearance, fillings and flavors.

CHOCOLATE RASPBERRY

SWEET MELISSA PÂTISSERIE // PG 186
Melissa's bite-sized cupcake features a super-moist and structured chocolate cake with a tart raspberry frosting. Need more? There's a fanciful flower on top.

VANILLA WITH VANILLA BUTTERCREAM

MAGNOLIA BAKERY // PG 27
A classic vanilla cupcake, like the one Grandma made in the days when no one was afraid of butter or sugar. The yellow cake is moist and mild; the frosting, crammed with so much sugar it will kick-start your heart.

YELLOW DAISY CUPCAKE

BILLY'S BAKERY // PG 109
This is a homey and tasty vanilla cupcake. The cake itself is firm with mild flavor, and you can see little dots of vanilla bean throughout. The buttercream is quite smooth and not too sweet, with colorful sprinkles on top.

RED VELVET CUPCAKE

BABYCAKES // PG 57
Let go of your usual cupcake expectations and you might be pleasantly surprised by the vegan red velvet cupcake. It's crumbly and dense, with a creamy vanilla frosting.

SIMPLY YELLOW CAKE WITH MOCHA

AMY'S BREAD // PG 14
This cupcake has great coffee kick in its smooth, not-too-sweet mocha buttercream. The yellow cake is moist and flavorful.

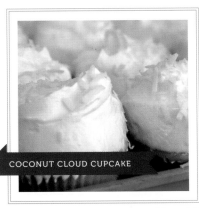

COCONUT CLOUD CUPCAKE

LITTLE CUPCAKE BAKESHOP // PG 83
This is a fantastically fluffy cupcake. The base is yellow cake, with Italian meringue mixed with coconut on top. It's like eating a cloud.

New York
Sweets

MIDTOWN AND UPTOWN

Over three hundred million cream puffs served!

BEARD PAPA'S

CREAM PUFFS FROM JAPAN

Yuji Hirota opened his first Beard Papa's in 1999 in Osaka, Japan. Although this is a worldwide chain, the Upper West Side location is a treat to behold. The spot is staffed with gracious Japanese ladies who will charm you with their giggling and their warm nature, but don't be fooled: they take their craft seriously. Beard Papa's bills itself as the "world's best cream puffs." Indeed, these confections fly off the shelves—and they simply float into your mouth. Start with the original vanilla cream puff to get an idea of what it's all about, then graduate to chocolate, coffee, or pumpkin. The strawberry cream puff, made with fresh fruit puree, is like no other. For a taste of Japan, try the green tea cream puff; homesick Brits should go for the Earl Grey cream puffs. My favorite is the cocoa puff, which is laced with dark chocolate chunks. In a fun twist, Beard Papa's lets you choose your own filling. The cream custard, the base of all the puffs, takes more than two hours to make and is made several times throughout the day, so everything is as fresh as can be. Each puff is served artistically on a small plate, so to get the full effect of these puffs, it is best to eat in.

2167 BROADWAY
NEW YORK, NY
10024
212-799-3770
....

MUGINOHOINTL.COM

BETH'S FARM KITCHEN

HANDMADE JAMS AND JELLIES

UNION SQUARE
GREEN MARKET
800-331-5267
....

BETHSFARM
KITCHEN.COM

Beth Linskey started her jam and chutney business thirty-one years ago in her Upper West Side apartment, and she has made literally tons of jams and jellies since. She's now based in Stuyvesant Falls, New York, and sells her products at the Union Square Greenmarket. I visited the operation upstate, and the drive up the Hudson Valley is magical: rolling hills, big sky, cows, goats, and huge pastures as far as the eye can see. The aroma from Beth's suddenly wafts through the air, and you know you have arrived. In an 1850s-era farmhouse in Columbia County, big pots of jams and jellies boil on the stove as "the ladies" peel and chop and chat about family and friends. Beth started with strawberry jam and has since developed ninety-plus flavors of jams, jellies, and chutneys. Her current favorites are Cherrycot, a marriage of cherry and apricot, and Raspyboyberry, a combination of raspberries and blackberries. But her best-seller is the strawberry-rhubarb. The table at the Greenmarket is laden with open jars of jams for tasting. You might get sticky, but that's OK, because every flavor is finger-licking great. Beth is as sweet as her jams, and she's always willing to give her customers a lesson or two. My favorite flavor is the Triple Orange Marmalade, made from, you guessed it, oranges, grapefruits, and lemons. Pucker up and enjoy!

Aunt Gilda's Plum Crumb Cake

MAKES 6 TO 8 SERVINGS

FROM THE KITCHEN OF BETH'S FARM KITCHEN

1½ CUPS ALL-PURPOSE FLOUR

½ CUP SUGAR

1 TEASPOON BAKING POWDER

¼ CUP (1 STICK) UNSALTED BUTTER, SOFTENED, PLUS MORE FOR THE PAN

1 CUP CHOPPED WALNUTS (OPTIONAL)

1 LARGE EGG, BEATEN

1 CUP BETH'S FARM KITCHEN PLUM JAM

1. Preheat the oven to 400°F. Butter an 8-inch square baking pan.

2. In a large bowl, combine the flour, sugar, and baking powder, then cut in the butter until a fine crumb forms. Stir in the walnuts, if using. With fork, stir in the egg until large crumbs form. Leave the mixture loose, and don't overmix.

3. Divide the crumb mixture into two equal portions. Firmly press one portion of crumb into the bottom and up the sides of the prepared pan. Spread the jam on top of the crumb layer. Sprinkle the second portion of the crumb mixture on top of the jam layer, leaving the crumbs loose. Bake for 15 minutes (you may want to place a baking sheet on the rack below the pan so any drippings don't burn on the bottom of the oven), then lower the oven temperature to 350°F and bake for 40 to 45 minutes longer, until golden brown. Let cool completely on a wire rack so the cake will set. Cut into squares and serve.

This is a family recipe of Liz Beals, the chief jam maker at Beth's Farm Kitchen.

DON'T MISS:
Chocolate Icebox
Cake

Peanut Butter
Chocolate Chip

Oatmeal Raisin
Cookie

Pea

BILLY'S BAKERY
OLD-FASHIONED ALL-AMERICAN TREATS

If you need a pick-me-up, go to Billy's Bakery—it's hard to be unhappy inside a place that makes cupcakes, cakes, bars, and cookies in so many flavors and choices. It's a race to the senses as soon as you walk in the door: Will your eyes widen at the cupcake display first, or will your nose catch the amazing aroma of baking wafting from the ovens? The down-home decor is a throwback to the 1950s, and Billy's bakers are always ready with a smile and a suggestion for their favorite sweet. For me, although the cupcakes are a little bite of heaven, just thinking about the first bite of the chocolate icebox cake gives me goose bumps. If you like fresh whipped cream layered between chocolate wafers, than this is the choice for you—it's the ultimate combination of fluff and crunch. Billy's was opened in 2003 with the idea that baking good, old-fashioned American classics with the freshest and best ingredients would be a winner, and it definitely is.

Plaza Food Hall
ONE WEST 59TH ST.
CONCOURSE LEVEL
NY, NY 10019
646-755-3221
....

Chelsea
184 NINTH AVENUE
NY, NY 10011
212-647-9956
....

Nolita
268 ELIZABETH ST.
NY, NY 10012
212-219-9956
....

Tribeca
75 FRANKLIN ST.
NY, NY 10013
212-647-9958
....

BILLYSBAKERY
NYC.COM

THE ORIGIN OF CHOCOLATE

CHOCOLATE IS MADE FROM THE BEANS OF THE PODS OF A PLANT NAMED THEOBROMA CACAO. THE PLANT WAS FIRST DOMESTICATED IN SOUTH AMERICA NEAR THE AMAZON BASIN APPROXIMATELY 4,000 YEARS AGO. THE EARLIEST KNOWN CULINARY USE OF CHOCOLATE OCCURRED IN SOUTHERN MEXICO AROUND 1,000 B.C. HERE IS WHERE IT IS BELIEVED CHOCOLATE WAS FIRST MADE INTO A DRINK.

Billy's Chocolate Cupcakes

FROM THE KITCHEN OF BILLY'S BAKERY

FOR THE CUPCAKES

2 CUPS SUGAR

2 CUPS ALL-PURPOSE FLOUR

½ TEASPOON BAKING POWDER

¾ CUP GHIRARDELLI UNSWEETENED COCOA POWDER

1 TEASPOON SALT

2 LARGE EGGS

¾ CUP MILK

½ CUP CANOLA OIL

1 TEASPOON PURE VANILLA EXTRACT

¾ CUP BREWED COFFEE, COOLED

FOR THE CHOCOLATE BUTTERCREAM ICING

½ CUP (1 STICK) UNSALTED BUTTER

⅔ CUP GHIRARDELLI UNSWEETENED COCOA POWDER

2½ CUPS CONFECTIONERS' SUGAR, OR MORE IF NEEDED

6 TABLESPOONS MILK, OR MORE IF NEEDED

2 TABLESPOONS PURE VANILLA EXTRACT

MAKE THE CUPCAKES

1. Preheat the oven to 325°F. Line cupcake tins with paper liners.

2. In a large bowl, stir together the sugar, flour, baking powder, cocoa powder, and salt.

3. In a large measuring cup, whisk the eggs, milk, oil, and vanilla together. Pour the egg mixture into the dry ingredients and beat with an electric mixer on high speed for about 3 minutes, until well incorporated. Beat in the coffee. Spoon the batter into the cupcake tins, filling each half to two thirds full.

4. Bake for 25 to 30 minutes, until a toothpick inserted in the center of a cupcake comes out clean. Let cool slightly in the tins, then remove the cupcakes to wire racks to cool completely.

MAKE THE ICING

1. Melt the butter in a small saucepan, then remove from the heat. Stir in the cocoa powder until smooth. Alternating with the milk and vanilla, gradually sprinkle in the confectioners' sugar, stirring after each addition until smooth. If the frosting is too runny, add more confectioners' sugar. If it is too stiff, add a little more milk.

2. Spread the icing on the cooled cupcakes with a knife, using as much or as little icing as you like. Then, of course, you can lick the bowl!

EATALY

EMPORIUM OF AUTHENTIC ITALIAN TREATS

200 FIFTH AVENUE
NEW YORK, NY
10010
212-229-2560
....
EATALYNY.COM

Standing in the middle of Eataly is like standing at the threshold of the Metropolitan Museum of Art. The big question is: Where do you go first? You are beckoned visually to every corner of the store. For me, the sweets counters, including the pastries, gelato, and sorbet areas, are paramount. Everything in the store is Italian, starting with its founder and creator, Oscar Farinetti, who opened Eataly in Turin in 2007. Mario Batali and Joe Bastianich then helped him bring Eataly to New York City. This food emporium serves those who want to host a banquet, create a romantic dinner for two, or just take an indulgent break in the day for a coffee and something sweet. The choices are plentiful—and it is hard to choose! The good news is, Luca Montersino has perfected the art of healthy pastry by creating a line of *dolce* (sweets) called *golosi di salute*, or flavors of health. There are no artificial colors, preservatives, hydrogenated fats, or refined oils, and some are even gluten- and sugar-free. There are round pastries made of rice flour and filled with white, milk, and dark chocolates, and square pastries with fruit that's been soaked in Moscato. There are chocolate mousse sandwiches with meringue, rice flour, sponge cake, and vanilla Chantilly cream. There's tiramisu with honey and hazelnut nougat. The list goes on. And the spoon sweets come in these adorable little covered containers—I love to buy a bunch for a dinner party so guests can choose their own. My favorite treat is the Panna Cotta Alla Vaniglia: Orange salted caramel topped with *panna cotta* and streusel pieces—and it's gluten-free! Although the patrons who fill Eataly from dawn until dusk are from all over the world, the atmosphere is unmistakably Italian.

DON'T MISS
Panna Cotta Alla
Vaniglia

ELENI'S

PICTURE-PERFECT ICED COOKIES

**Upper East
Side**

1266 MADISON
AVENUE
NEW YORK, NY
10128
888-435-3647

....

**Chelsea
Market**

75 NINTH AVENUE
NEW YORK, NY
10011
212-255-7990

....

ELENIS.COM

If you want to buy treats for a special occasion—be it a
baby shower, a birthday party, or as a thank you—or if you
love shoes, handbags, flowers, or butterflies, then Eleni's
handmade iced cookies are for you. Eleni Gianopulos
moved to New York City almost twenty-five years ago
from Northern California. What started as a small catering
business featuring her mother's famous oatmeal raisin
cookie recipe soon turned into an iced-cookie empire.
The selection is endless. Eleni has thought of every
possible cookie shape and uses a palette of colors that
would make Renoir proud. The flavors include Beyond
Butterscotch, Ginger Snappy, Single Sensation, Pink Sugar,
Milk and Cookies, and, of course, chocolate chip, oatmeal
chocolate chip, and many more. And although her
cookies are what made her famous, the array of cupcakes
is also quite impressive. They boast names like Manhattan,
5th Avenue, Black and White, Pretty in Pink, Vanilla-Vanilla,
and the favorite of all favorites, red velvet. Eleni's cookies
are not just cookies—they're a way to say something
special to the lucky recipient.

EMPIRE CAKE

ELEGANT ALL-AMERICAN CREATIONS

Empire is located at Eighth Avenue and Fifteenth Street, where the West Village, Chelsea, and the Meatpacking District meet. If you are so inclined, grab your honey, a bottle of wine, and a few sweets from Empire Cake, then walk over to the Highline, the elevated railroad-turned-park, to watch the sunset. The choice of cakes is endless, but let me tempt you with some favorites: vanilla cream cake with vanilla buttercream, German chocolate cake with coconut-pecan filling, red velvet cake, carrot cake, *dulce de leche* cake, and oh, my goodness, the salted caramel chocolate cake with dark chocolate ganache. The uniqueness of this bakery lies not only in its gourmet cakes, but also in its snack cakes, including its Swiss Roll (a chocolate cake rolled with vanilla cream and ganache, then dipped in chocolate), Chocolate Covered Snowballs, Passion Fruit (yellow cake with passion fruit curd filling, dipped in white chocolate and sprinkled with coconut), and Brooklyn Blackout (with chocolate pudding filling). The list just keeps on going, and it only gets creamier, sweeter, and more delicious. The cookie selection changes daily, but the 8th Avenue is my favorite: a gluten-free cookie made with almond flour, dried fruit, and nuts. Others include a heart-shaped black-and-white, thumbprint cookies, and coconut macaroons. Everything here is a winner and, simply put, Empire is on the rise.

112 EIGHTH AVENUE
NEW YORK, NY
10011
212-242-5858
. . . .
EMPIRECAKE.COM

French Vanilla Sablés

FROM THE KITCHEN OF BEURRE & SEL

FOR THE COOKIES

2 STICKS (16 TABLESPOONS; 8 OUNCES) UNSALTED BUTTER, AT ROOM TEMPERATURE

½ CUP SUGAR

¼ CUP CONFECTIONERS' SUGAR, SIFTED

½ TEASPOON SALT, PREFERABLY SEA SALT

2 LARGE EGG YOLKS, AT ROOM TEMPERATURE

2 TEASPOONS PURE VANILLA EXTRACT

2 CUPS ALL-PURPOSE FLOUR

FOR DECORATING (OPTIONAL)

1 EGG YOLK

SANDING SUGAR

In France, sablés, rich, tender shortbread cookies, are as beloved as chocolate-chip cookies are in America. They have a paradoxical but paradisiacal texture—both crumbly and melt-in-your-mouth.

MAKE THE SUGAR COOKIES

1. Working in a mixer fitted with the paddle attachment (or by hand in a bowl with a rubber spatula), beat the butter at medium speed until it is smooth and very creamy. Add the granulated and confectioners' sugars as well as the salt and continue to beat until well blended, about 1 minute. The mixture should be smooth and velvety, not fluffy and airy. Reduce the mixer speed to low and, one by one, beat in the yolks, then the vanilla, again beating until the mixture is homogenous.

2. Turn off the mixer, pour in the flour, drape a kitchen towel over the mixer to protect yourself from flying flour, and pulse the mixer about 5 times, pulsing at low speed for a second or two each time. Take a peek—if there is still a lot of flour on the surface of the dough, pulse a couple of times more; if not, remove the towel. Continuing to work at low speed, mix for about 30 seconds more, just until the flour disappears into the dough and the dough looks uniformly moist. (If most of the flour is incorporated but you've still got some on the bottom of the bowl, use a rubber spatula to work the rest of the flour into the dough.) The dough will not clean the sides of the bowl nor will it come together in a ball—and it shouldn't. You want to work the dough as little as possible. What you're aiming for is a soft, moist, clumpy (rather than smooth) dough. Pinch it and it will feel a little like Play-doh.

3. Scrape the dough out onto a smooth work surface, gather it into a ball and divide it in half. Shape each piece into a smooth log about 9 inches long (it's easiest to work on a piece of plastic wrap and use the plastic to help form the log). Wrap the logs well and chill them for at least 3 hours, preferably longer—the dough can be kept in the refrigerator for up to 3 days or frozen for up to 2 months.

GETTING READY TO BAKE THE COOKIES

1. Center a rack in the oven and preheat the oven to 350°F. Line a baking sheet with parchment paper or a silicone mat.

TO DECORATE AND BAKE:

1. Remove a log of dough from the refrigerator and place it on a piece of parchment or wax paper. Whisk the yolk until it is smooth and brush some of the yolk all over the sides of the dough—this is the glue—then sprinkle the entire surface of the log with sugar. Trim the ends of the roll if they're ragged and slice the log into ⅓-inch thick cookies. (You can make these as thick as ½ inch or as thin as—but no thinner than—¼ inch.)

2. Place the rounds on the baking sheet, leaving an inch of spread space between each cookie, and bake for 17 to 20 minutes, rotating the baking sheet at the halfway point. (It's best to bake only one sheet a time.) When properly baked, the cookies will be light brown on the bottom, lightly golden around the edges and pale on top; they may feel tender when you touch the top gently and that's fine. Pull the baking sheet from the oven and let the cookies rest a minute or two before carefully lifting them onto a rack with a wide metal spatula and allowing them to cool to room temperature.

3. Repeat with the remaining log of dough, making sure the baking sheet is cool before you bake the second batch.

STORING

1. The cookies will keep in a tin at room temperature for about 5 days. If you do not trim the sablés with sugar, they can be wrapped airtight and frozen for up to 2 months. Because the sugar will melt in the freezer, decorated cookies are not suitable for freezing.

KALUSTYAN'S
EXOTIC FLAVORS OF THE WORLD

Opened in 1944 by Mr. K. Kalustyan, Kalustyan's is an Indian food emporium on Lexington Avenue in Murray Hill. After Mr. Kalustyan passed away, the shop was taken over by Marhaba International, Inc., who expanded the grocery store into a treasure trove of food from all over the world. The focus is on Middle Eastern sweets, dried fruits, nuts, and pastries. Walk the aisles and enjoy the exotic smells and sights. Try dates from Jordan, goji berries from the Himalayas, Persian green raisins from Iran, guavas from South Africa, red dates from China, or nectarines from California. If you want something more sophisticated, check out the vast selection of candied glazed fruit, including glazed apricots from Australia, candied chestnuts from Turkey, crystallized ginger from Thailand, and glazed orange peel from Italy. The perfect complement to fruit is nuts—try sugar-coated almonds from Jordan, silver-coated almonds from France, and perhaps some candied fennel seeds from India. You will leave the store feeling exhausted but visually satiated. After all, you've just taken a trip around the world.

KALUSTYANS.COM
123 LEXINGTON AVENUE ∾ NEW YORK, NY 10016 ∾ 212-685-3451

BEURRE & SEL
THE PATH TO WORLD PEACE

Dorie Greenspan is a legend of our time—the author of ten cookbooks and winner of six James Beard Awards. Dorie and her charming son Joshua decided to open Beurre & Sel in 2012, encouraged by the success of a series of cookie pop-up shops they had collaborated on in recent years. The name comes from the fact that Dorie considers butter and salt to be the most vital ingredients in making great cookies. These cookies are baked in rings and a smaller size is packaged in plastic tubes. All of their melt-in-your-mouth creations will have your inner cookie monster screaming for joy. But my favorite is the streusel-topped jammer, which oozes with flavor and offers several different textures in each bite. There are other delicious choices such as Coconut-Lime; Espresso-Chocolate Chunkers with chocolate chips, cherries, and cashews; French Vanilla Sablés, a crumbly butter cookie (sablé literally means "sandy"); and World Peace Cookies, which are based on a chocolate sable taught to Dorie by Pierre Hermé. In Dorie's house they are called World Peace Cookies because she says, "if everyone had these cookies there'd be peace in the world." This is a cookie emporium par excellence.

WWW.BEURREANDSEL.COM
UPTOWN LA MARQUETA ∾ 1607 PARK AVENUE ∾ NY, NY 10029
LOWER EAST SIDE 120 ESSEX STREET ∾ NY, NY 10002 ∾ 917-737-1818

LA MAISON DU CHOCOLAT
AN EXQUISITE BOUTIQUE

It is no surprise to find La Maison du Chocolat while strolling up Madison Avenue and passing the shops of every famous designer you can think of. The store is fitted with cabinets that look like jewelry showcases. The staff is elegantly dressed and presents the chocolates as carefully as if they were diamonds and pearls. Robert Linxe, the master chocolatier behind the business, opened his first shop in Paris in 1955 and, fortunately for all of us chocolate aficionados, graced the Upper East Side with his creations at this gorgeous shop and café in 1990. The cocoa beans come from Venezuela, Trinidad, Ecuador, and Madagascar. The ganache is smooth as silk, the pralines are a crunchy ambrosia, and the fruit-filled chocolates with coconut, lemon zest, raspberry, and pistachio are beyond description. Although seeing is believing—and tasting is even better—there's no reason to stop at just the chocolates. The éclairs, ice cream, and sablé cookies will have you swooning!

LAMAISONDUCHOCOLAT.COM
UPPER EAST SIDE 1018 MADISON AVENUE ~ NY, NY 10075 ~ 212-744-7117
MIDTOWN 30 ROCKEFELLER PLAZA ~ NY, NY 10112 ~ 212-265-9404
FINANCIAL DISTRICT 63 WALL STREET ~ NY, NY 10005 ~ 212-952-1123
PLAZA FOOD HALL ONE WEST 58TH STREET ~ NY, NY 10019 ~ 212-355-3436

POSEIDON BAKERY
SWEETS FROM THE OLD COUNTRY

The Poseidon Bakery, in the Hell's Kitchen neighborhood, was founded in 1923, and it's still making its delicious Greek sweets today. This third-generation bakery, now run by Lili Fable and her son Paul, is a charming throwback with its blue-and-white decor. The staff is there to greet you with a smile and patiently explain the entire menu of Greek treats. The homemade baklava, layered with chopped almonds and walnuts and drenched in honey, are light, crisp, and best-selling. If you're on the go and the baklava sounds a bit sticky for you, then get the *saragli*, basically rolled baklava, which is easier to munch while you're in motion. If you aren't a baklava fan at all (although I don't know how that is possible), give the *revani*, a fluffy almond cake, a shot. The *galaktoboureko*, layers of phyllo dough with a cream filling, joins the wonderful selection of cookies always on display. Other selections include *finikia*, a crushed walnut–and-almond cookie dipped in honey, and pastelli, sesame candy with almonds and pistachios. To complete the Poseidon adventure, try an apple, sour cherry, apricot, prune, cherry-cheese or pineapple-cheese strudel.

629 NINTH AVENUE ~ NEW YORK, NY 10036 ~ 212-757-6173

Almond-Oat Lace Cookies

FROM THE KITCHEN OF *BON APPETIT*

½ CUP WHOLE NATURAL, UNSALTED ALMONDS WITH SKINS

2 TABLESPOONS OLD-FASHIONED OATS

6 TABLESPOONS UNSALTED BUTTER

6 TABLESPOONS SUPERFINE SUGAR

2 TABLESPOONS PACKED LIGHT BROWN SUGAR

1½ TEASPOONS HONEY

1 TABLESPOON ALL-PURPOSE FLOUR

¼ TEASPOON KOSHER SALT

4 OUNCES BITTERSWEET CHOCOLATE, MELTED

1. Preheat the oven to 350°F and arrange racks in the lower and upper thirds of the oven. Line two rimless baking sheets with parchment paper.

2. Pulse the almonds and oats in a food processor until a coarse meal forms. Set aside.

3. Melt the butter in a medium saucepan over medium heat.

4. Add both sugars and the honey and whisk until blended and the sugar dissolves, 1 to 2 minutes. Remove from the heat.

5. Add the almond mixture, flour, and salt; stir until well combined.

6. Spoon the batter by 2-teaspoon portions onto the baking sheets, spacing them 2½ inches apart. Using your fingertips, pat the cookies down to ¼-inch-high rounds; push in any jagged edges to form smooth circles.

7. Bake, rotating the baking sheets after 6 minutes, until dark golden brown and the cookies have spread out into a thin layer, 10 to 12 minutes. Slide the cookies, still on the parchment, onto wire racks and let cool completely.

8. Using a pastry brush, brush half of each cookie with melted chocolate.

9. Let stand until the chocolate is set, about 2 hours.

10. The cookies can be made up to 2 days ahead. Store in an airtight container between sheets of parchment or waxed paper.

GLASER'S BAKE SHOP

A YORKVILLE LEGEND

Glaser's opened in 1902, and more than a century later, this family-run bakery is still going strong. Third-generation bakers John and Herbert Glaser carry on the Glaser tradition in the same premises at First Avenue and Eighty-Seventh Street in the Yorkville neighborhood. Regular customers are treated like extended family and known by name. Children walk in with their mothers and point to their favorite cookie as they squeal with delight. The shop, a throwback to a much earlier time, is notable for its fine wood cabinetry with huge glass doors filled with trays of warm baked goods fresh from the oven. Time has stood still here, so do not rush your visit. Enjoy the old-fashioned personal service that you've heard your grandparents speak of. The choice of baked goods is mesmerizing. There are sugar-dusted jelly doughnuts, apple turnovers, French crullers, Linzer tarts, and muffins in assorted flavors. Danish pastries, coffee rings, puff pastries, and assorted butter cookies are made from the original Glaser recipes and taste as good as they did in 1902. You know the saying: If it ain't broke, don't fix it. While you are waiting your turn, breathe in the aroma of freshly baked cinnamon buns, crumb buns, and pound cakes. My favorite are the oversize, moist black-and-white cookies, which bring me right back to my childhood.

1670 FIRST AVENUE
NEW YORK, NY
10128
212-289-2562
....
GLASERS
BAKESHOP.COM

L.A. BURDICK CHOCOLATE SHOP & CAFÉ

FANCIFUL BONBONS AND COZY CAFÉ

5 EAST 20TH
STREET
NEW YORK, NY
10003
212-796-0143
....
BURDICK
CHOCOLATE.COM

If I told you I had just bitten the head off a mouse, munched through a penguin, and was about to eat a handful of bees, would you think I was in a chocolate store? L.A. Burdick Chocolate on Twentieth Street in the Flatiron district makes all of these charming items, both for sale in its café and as favors for parties and other events. Chocolatier Larry Burdick opened his shop in 1987, and with Michael Klug, his chocolate and pastry chef, he creates artisanal chocolates to delight and satisfy discerning chocolate lovers. The chocolate is imported from France, Switzerland, and Venezuela, and it contains no artificial colors or preservatives. Cut and shaped by hand, bonbons come in dreamy flavors like lemongrass with peppercorn, Earl Grey, cashew, and sesame. The chocolate-dipped apricots, citrus peels, pears, and ginger are an exotic departure from the traditional, but if chocolate isn't your fancy—hard to imagine!—marzipan, nougat, and *pâtes de fruits* are also on offer. The chocolate salted caramels are irresistible, and the *pavés glacé* are spectacular.

Sweets Sampler: Chocolate

SIMULTANEOUSLY SENSUAL, ELEGANT AND NOSTALGIC, sometimes a bite of chocolate is all it takes to turn the day around. Make that one bite a good one, with these chocolatiers.

PAYS DE SAINT MALO

MAISON DU CHOCOLATE // PG 123
This is the Cary Grant of chocolates: smooth and elegant. The creamy ganache center is blended with caramel and has a hint of salt. It perfectly complements its milk chocolate exterior.

CRÈME BRULEE

KEE'S CHOCOLATE // PG 123
A hand-molded chocolate, this has a smooth, mild custard interior against a strong backdrop of dark chocolate.

CHAMPAGNE TRUFFLE

JACQUES TORRES // PG 123
A milk chocolate exterior, with cream and Taittinger champagne on the inside. The champagne flavor is addictive!

CHOCOLATE BACON TRUFFLES

VOSGES // PG 123
These are both savory and sweet, topped with hickory smoked bacon pieces that make a unique contrast to the dark chocolate and creamy interior.

ALMONDS & SEA SALT BAR

MAST BROS. // PG 123
This is a dark, bitter and salty chocolate bar. Eaten slowly, the fruit of the chocolate gradually emerges, especially in contrast to the bite of salt and the toasty nuts.

PB&J

BOND STREET CHOCOLATES // PG 123
It's like a sandwich, only enrobed in dark chocolate instead of bread. Bite into it for a burst of jelly sweetness, mellowed out by salty, nutty peanut butter. It's better than any lunch mom ever made.

GANACHE BASICS

ANY DESSERT WITH GANACHE IS GOING TO BE A CHOCOLATE LOVER'S DREAM. MADE WITH CHOCOLATE AND CREAM, AND SOMETIMES BUTTER, THIS SWEET GLISTENING MIXTURE IS USED TO DECORATE DESSERTS, FILL CAKES AND PASTRIES, AND MAKE TRUFFLES. GANACHE MEANS "JOWL" IN FRENCH, AND THOUGH IT IS HARD TO FIGURE OUT WHAT GANACHE AND JOWLS HAVE IN COMMON, ITS FULL-ON CHOCOLATE LUSCIOUSNESS DEMANDS TO BE EATEN AND SAVORED (WITH MINIMAL EFFORT OF ONE'S JAW).

LA BERGAMOTE PATISSERIE

A QUICK TRIP TO PARIS

Why save your air miles to visit France when you can go there anytime you like by visiting La Bergamote on Ninth Avenue in Chelsea? Since 1998, Stephane Willemine, the shop's pastry chef, and Romain Lamaze, the managing director, have been one great team producing heavenly, decadent treats for all who enter their little corner of France in New York City. If you thought the age of the Concorde was dead, it is not so at La Bergamote. The patisserie's version consists of chocolate meringue, mousse, and dark chocolate shavings. Try not to eat it at supersonic speed, if you can—savoring it will make the journey longer. You do not need to get out your atlas to look for Magellan. Instead, look here for a creation of chocolate mousse, gingerbread biscuits, and chocolate ganache. And though the word *pompadour* may evoke images of a beautiful French woman, here it's a confection made of oranges, Grand Marnier, and chocolate mousse. The store is so full of gastronomic delights that the only problem is choosing among sweets like Trois Chocolats (a mousse of milk, dark, and white chocolates), coconut crème brûlée, and the Bergamotier (Bergamot mousse and chocolate caramel ganache). Take your time; there's much to consider, including colorful, mouthwatering mini fruit tarts, éclairs, napoleans, jellies, and pastries that would look at home in the Louvre. Forget the calories, live for the moment at this delightful shop, the haute couture of patisseries. *N'est-ce pas?*

Chelsea
177 NINTH AVENUE
NEW YORK, NY
10011
212-627-9010
....
Clinton
515 WEST 52ND
STREET
NEW YORK, NY
10019
212-586-2429
....
LABERGAMOTE
NYC.COM

LADURÉE NEW YORK

MACARON HEAVEN

864 MADISON AVE.
NEW YORK, NY
10021
646-558-3157
············
LADUREE.FR

Ladurée opened in Paris in 1862 and has seen several incarnations since, from bakery to tea salon to its current embodiment as a tearoom, pastry shop, restaurant, chocolate shop, and ice cream parlor. It has also gone international, thanks to the efforts of its current chairman, David Holder, which means New Yorkers get to enjoy one on Madison Avenue. One feels the need to dress up before entering this fine establishment—Mr. Holder has adhered to traditional values and practices, and it seems we should do the same as a mark of respect. Ladurée is known for its colorful *macaron*, and this is not your mother's macaroon. That was more like a Ping-Pong ball with strings of coconut dipped in chocolate. This is a French *macaron*, and it is light, airy, and filled with cream. The flavors change with the seasons, but I recommend a selection of red fruits, chocolate milk, cherry blossom, pure chocolate, or the *incroyable* strawberry. Other delicacies include cakes, éclairs, and tarts galore, in flavors like passion fruit and raspberry, lemon, praline, chocolate, and the infamous tarte tatin. You will definitely leave asking yourself why it is that French women don't get fat.

NEW YORK SWEETS
·····························

Salade de Fruits Rouges Menthole

MAKES 12 SERVINGS

FROM THE KITCHEN OF LADURÉE NEW YORK

FOR THE RED BERRY SYRUP

1½ CUPS WATER

¾ CUP GRANULATED SUGAR

¾ CUP RED CURRANTS

¾ CUP RASPBERRIES

15 FRESH MINT LEAVES

FOR THE FRUIT

3⅓ CUPS STRAWBERRIES
(GARIGUETTE, IF
POSSIBLE)

1 CUP RED CURRANTS

2 CUPS RASPBERRIES

1 CUP BLACKBERRIES

1 CUP BLUEBERRIES

MAKE THE RED BERRY SYRUP

1. In a saucepan, bring the water, sugar, currants, and raspberries to a boil.

2. Remove from the heat and add the mint. Cover and set aside to steep for 20 minutes.

3. Remove and discard the mint leaves.

4. Using an immersion blender, blend until smooth.

5. Pour the syrup through a fine-mesh sieve into a bowl and set aside.

PREPARE THE FRUIT

1. Wash, hull, and slice the strawberries.

2. Remove the stems from the currants.

3. Coat plates or fill individual bowls with the red berry syrup and arrange all the fruit in a decorative pattern over it. Keep in the refrigerator until ready to serve.

A TOKEN OF FRANCE

A BOX OF PASTEL-COLORED MACARONS IS CERTAINLY A LOVELY SIGHT TO BEHOLD—AND TASTY TO EAT. THESE MERINGUE-BASED SANDWICH COOKIES HAVE BEEN POPULAR IN FRANCE SINCE THE BEGINNING OF THE TWENTIETH CENTURY (THANK YOUS GO TO LADURÉE) BUT HAVE BECOME VERY POPULAR IN THE UNITED STATES AND OTHER COUNTRIES IN RECENT YEARS. THEY COME IN A MYRIAD OF FLAVORS AND COLORS. THE EXTERIORS ARE CRISP, THE INTERIORS SOFT, AND THEY HAVE A CREAMY FILLING, OFTEN OF VANILLA BUTTERCREAM, GANACHE, OR LEMON CURD. THESE TREATS ARE SO POPULAR IN FRANCE THAT MCDONALD'S SELLS THEM!

LADY M BOUTIQUE

THE ART OF THE CAKE

Upper East Side
41 EAST 78TH
STREET
NEW YORK, NY
10075
212-452-2222
....
Plaza Food Hall
ONE WEST 59TH ST.
NEW YORK, NY
10019
....
LADYM.COM

Lady M is known as the Tiffany of bakeries, and it is easy to see why. The cakes, tarts, and pies resemble beautiful jewels on display. Upon entering this fine establishment on Madison Avenue on the Upper East Side, even the most discerning of shoppers will do a double take. Every piece is a masterpiece in design, almost like sculptures on display in an art gallery. Fortunately, these cakes are real and edible, the exquisite creation of a team of Japanese chefs who take great pride in their masterful works of art. This bright, cozy, and inviting bakery beckons you to partake in an unforgettable feast of sweets. This is not something to be done in a hurry, and the clientele look like they are there to stay, dressed as they are in their finery. (The shop *is* located just a few steps off Madison Avenue, after all.) Lady M's signature Milles Crêpes cake is not comparable to anything else in the world. Imagine twenty paper-thin crepes layered with fresh Chantilly cream, light enough to cut with a feather. Perhaps the Banana Mille Feuille is more to your taste? Thin layers of the finest flaky pastry, combined with whipped cream, sponge cake, and bananas. As airy as it is, this cake is not to be taken lightly. The strawberry shortcake is in a league of its own with its perfectly placed strawberries and ethereal cake. But do not stop there. Try the chocolate, coconut, or green tea Mille Crêpes. If you have all afternoon, and, believe me, you will somehow find the time, move on to the flourless chocolate cake, coffee mousse cake, or *gâteau nuage*. Yes, it *is* as light as a cloud. No wonder the ladies who lunch linger in this jewel.

Lady M Mille Crêpes

Gâteau de Crêpes

INSPIRED BY LADY M BOUTIQUE

FOR THE CRÊPE BATTER

- 6 TABLESPOONS UNSALTED BUTTER
- 6 LARGE EGGS
- 1½ CUPS ALL-PURPOSE FLOUR
- 7 TABLESPOONS SUGAR

PINCH OF SALT

- 3 CUPS MILK, ROOM TEMPERATURE

FOR THE PASTRY CREAM

- 2 CUPS MILK
- 1 VANILLA BEAN, SPLIT AND SCRAPED
- 6 LARGE EGG YOLKS
- ½ CUP SUGAR
- ⅓ CUP CORNSTARCH, SIFTED
- 3½ TABLESPOONS UNSALTED BUTTER

TO ASSEMBLE

CORN OIL

- 2 CUPS HEAVY CREAM
- 1 TABLESPOON GRANULATED SUGAR, PLUS 2 TABLESPOONS MORE IF CARAMELIZING THE TOP
- 3 TABLESPOONS KIRSCH

CONFECTIONERS' SUGAR, FOR TOPPING

This is your chance to try to match the skill of Lady M's master bakers. We'll warn you now: This is not easy. The toughest part here is the dexterity required to stack one layer evenly on top of the next. Use a form and don't be afraid to use a sharp knife to trim the edges.

MAKE THE CRÊPE BATTER

1. In a small saucepan, cook the butter until brown, the color of hazelnuts. Set aside.

2. With a mixer on medium-low speed, beat together the eggs, flour, sugar, and salt. Slowly add the milk and browned butter. Pour into a container with a spout, cover, and refrigerate overnight.

MAKE THE PASTRY CREAM

1. In a saucepan, bring the milk with the vanilla bean and seeds to a boil, then remove from the heat and set aside for 10 minutes; remove the vanilla bean.

2. Fill a large bowl with ice and set aside a smaller bowl that can hold the finished pastry cream and be placed in this ice bath. In a medium-size heavy-bottomed saucepan, whisk the egg yolks, sugar, and cornstarch together. Gradually whisk in the hot milk, then place the pan over high heat and bring to a boil, whisking vigorously for 1 to 2 minutes.

3. Press the pastry cream through a fine-mesh sieve into the smaller bowl. Set the bowl in the ice bath and stir until the pastry cream cools to 140°F on an instant-read thermometer. Stir in the butter. When completely cool, cover and refrigerate overnight.

ASSEMBLE THE CAKE

1. Bring the batter to room temperature. Line a baking sheet with parchment paper. Place a nonstick or well-seasoned 9-inch crêpe pan over medium heat. Swab the surface with oil on a paper towel, then add about 3 tablespoons of the batter and swirl to cover the surface.

2. Cook until the bottom just begins to brown, about 1 minute, then carefully lift an edge and flip the crêpe with your fingers. Cook on the other side for no longer than 5 seconds. Flip the crêpe onto the prepared baking sheet. Repeat until you have 20 perfect crêpes.

3. Press the pastry cream through a sieve into a bowl once more. Whip the heavy cream together with the granulated sugar and kirsch until thick; it won't hold peaks. Fold the whipped cream into the pastry cream.

4. Lay 1 crêpe on a cake plate. Using an icing spatula, completely cover the crêpe with a thin layer of pastry cream (about ¼ cup). Cover with a second crêpe and repeat to make a stack of 20, with the best-looking crêpe on top.

5. Chill in the refrigerator for at least 2 hours.

6. Let the cake sit at room temperature for 30 minutes before serving. Dust with confectioners' sugar. Slice like a cake and serve.

LEVAIN BAKERY
GENEROUS AND HOMEY TREATS

Upper West Side

167 WEST 74TH
STREET
NEW YORK, NY
10023
212-874-6080
....

Harlem

2167 FREDERICK
DOUGLASS BLVD.
NEW YORK, NY
10026
646-455-0952
....

LEVAINBAKERY.COM

Levain Bakery is nestled in the heart of New York City's Upper West Side. This small shop oftentimes has a line out the door of not only neighborhood regulars but also people from all over the world who have heard about the legendary baked goods, especially the shop's famous six-ounce chocolate chip walnut cookie. The bakery was founded in 1994 by friends Connie McDonald and Pam Weekes. Connie was in banking and Pam was in fashion, and both were competitive swimmers who were training together for the Ironman. Their workouts left them hungry for great food, and thus began passionate discussions about creating the world's best chocolate chip cookie. Following that masterstroke, the duo devised their oatmeal raisin cookie, dark chocolate chocolate chip cookie, and dark chocolate peanut butter cookie. The cookies are extraordinary right out of the oven at the store, but they're also delicious once you've brought them home, with a quart of milk to dip them into. Cookies aside, the blueberry muffin is almost all muffin top, and the chocolate chip brioche, bursting with chips, is high on my list of favorites. I can never decide between the *bomboloncini* (small jelly doughnut) and the raisin sticky bun, so I usually get them both and indulge. Levain recently opened an outpost in Harlem, and it also does the Hamptons a favor by baking its yummy goods on Long Island.

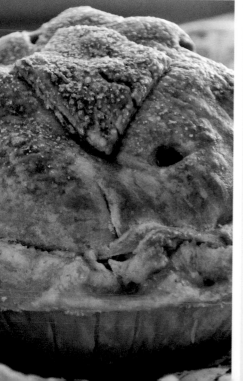

LITTLE PIE COMPANY

A CLASSIC & UNBEATABLE REPERTOIRE

The Little Pie Company on West Forty-Third Street has been selling pleasure in the form of pies since 1985. Owners Arnold Wilkerson and Michael Deraney have found success by baking pies the way their grandmothers did. They grew up in California and the Midwest, respectively, but in both cases, their grandmothers taught them how to pick fruit and make the perfect piecrust—a coincidence that has helped make the Little Pie Company into what it is today. The aroma wafting down the street draws you in to the shop. All of the pies and cakes are pure, fresh, and delicious, with nothing artificial. The fruit pies are not overly sweet, so you're reminded of the tangy fresh fruit that goes into them. Savor a slice of the legendary sour cream-apple-walnut pie, made with Granny Smith apples, fresh sour cream, brown sugar, cinnamon, and walnut streusel. A taste of the three berry pie is a must—it's a luscious combination of strawberries, blueberries, and raspberries. The entire roster of pies (cherry, pecan, key lime, and many others), as well as the banana nut bread, the lemon pound cake, and the statutory New York cheesecake, will leave you wanting more. Thank you, Grandma!

424 WEST 43RD
STREET
NEW YORK, NY
10036
212-736-4780
....

LITTLEPIE
COMPANY.COM

Cherry Pie

FROM THE KITCHEN OF LITTLE PIE COMPANY

FOR THE OLD-FASHIONED DOUGH

- 2½ CUPS UNBLEACHED ALL-PURPOSE FLOUR
- I TABLESPOON SUGAR
- I TEASPOON SALT
- ½ CUP (I STICK) UNSALTED BUTTER, CHILLED AND CUT INTO 1-INCH PIECES FOR HAND MIXING METHOD; FROZEN AND CUT INTO 1-INCH PIECES FOR FOOD PROCESSOR METHOD
- ½ CUP VEGETABLE SHORTENING, CHILLED AND CUT INTO 1-INCH PIECES FOR HAND MIXING METHOD; FROZEN AND CUT INTO 1-INCH PIECES FOR FOOD PROCESSOR METHOD
- I LARGE EGG, BEATEN
- ¼ CUP VERY COLD WATER (REFRIGERATED OR CHILLED WITH ICE CUBES THAT ARE REMOVED BEFORE MEASURING)

MAKE THE OLD-FASHIONED DOUGH

The hand mixing method:

1. In a large bowl, whisk the flour, sugar, and salt together. Add the butter. Using your fingertips or a pastry blender, work the butter into the flour until the mixture forms pieces the size of peas. Add the shortening and cut it into the flour with a pastry blender.

2. Combine the egg and cold water. While stirring lightly with a fork, add the egg mixture to the flour-fat mixture in a fast, steady stream. Continue stirring, occasionally cleaning off the dough that collects on the tines of the fork, until the flour is almost completely mixed in but the dough does not form a ball. Turn the dough out onto a work surface.

3. Work in the unincorporated flour using the heel of your hand to press and push the dough just until it holds together. This is not kneading. Shape the dough into a 6-inch disc. There should be many small pieces of butter and shortening visible. Wrap the dough tightly in plastic wrap or waxed paper and refrigerate for at least 2 hours or overnight.

The food processor method:

1. Put the flour, sugar, and salt in a food processor fitted with the steel blade. Pulse twice to combine. Add the frozen pieces of butter and process for 8 seconds, until the butter is the size of large peas. Add the frozen shortening and pulse several times to cut it into the flour.

2. In a liquid measuring cup, combine the egg and cold water. Turn on the food processor and immediately add the egg mixture, taking about 5 seconds to pour it in. Process for an additional 5 seconds. Scrape down the sides and bottom of the bowl to help incorporate the flour more evenly. Process for another 5 seconds. Not all the flour will be incorporated; this is okay. Turn the dough out onto a work surface.

3. Work in the unincorporated flour using the heel of your hand to press and push the dough just until it holds together. This is not kneading. Shape the dough into a 6-inch disc. There should be many tiny flecks of butter and shortening visible. Wrap the dough tightly in plastic wrap or waxed paper and refrigerate for at least 2 hours or overnight.

FOR THE PIE

- 6 CUPS FROZEN PITTED MONTMORENCY CHERRIES

- 1⅛ CUPS SUGAR, PLUS ADDITIONAL FOR SPRINKLING ON THE LATTICE STRIPS

- ¼ CUP INSTANT TAPIOCA

- 1 TEASPOON FRESHLY SQUEEZED LEMON JUICE

- 1 LARGE EGG BEATEN WITH 3 TABLESPOONS COLD WATER

- VANILLA ICE CREAM, IF DESIRED

MAKE THE PIE

1. In a large bowl, combine the cherries and sugar. Let stand until the cherries are thawed, stirring gently every once in a while. Drain the cherries in a colander, reserving the juice. There will be about 1¼ cups juice. Check the thawed fruit for whole or partial cherry pits; discard them. Put the cherries in a large bowl and set aside.

2. In a small nonaluminum saucepan, stir together the reserved juice and the tapioca and let stand for 5 minutes. Then, over medium heat, stirring frequently, bring the mixture to a full boil. Remove the pan from the heat and stir in the lemon juice.

3. Pour the hot cherry juice mixture over the cherries and gently stir them together. Cover the bowl and refrigerate until thoroughly chilled, about 2 hours. Preheat the oven to 425°F.

4. Divide the dough in half. Roll out one half to fit a 9-inch pie plate. Line the pie plate with the dough and pour the filling into it.

5. For the lattice top, on a lightly floured surface, roll out the remaining dough half into a 13-inch circle and cut twelve 1-inch-wide lattice strips. Brush the lattice strips with the egg wash and sprinkle them with sugar. Arrange the strips over the filling.

6. Trim the bottom crust edge and the strips to a 1-inch overhang. Fold the bottom crust edge up over the lattice strips to form a thick edge, then flute the edges decoratively, pressing them together with your thumb and forefinger. Bake for 20 minutes, then lower the oven temperature to 350°F and continue to bake for an additional 40 minutes, or until the pastry is browned and the juices are bubbling. Let cool completely on a wire rack. Serve at room temperature, with vanilla ice cream on the side, if desired.

DEEP MOUNTAIN MAPLE
GIFTS FROM THE TREES

Howard and Stephanie Cantor have been producing maple syrup in Vermont's Northeast Kingdom since 1985. As they say, "There is no activity that ties one to nature as much as sugaring." The sap flows through the maple trees, then makes its way, via the Cantors, 350 miles to the Union Square Greenmarket, where for more than twenty-five years they've been bringing New York City some of the best maple syrup, candy, and sugar around. They live and work in the town of West Glover, Vermont, twenty-five miles from the Canadian border, with their three sons. Their land is dotted with maple, fir, and spruce trees overlooking Parker Pond. They sell syrup in raspberry and ginger flavors, but of course there are gallons upon gallons of maple for the purists. Deep Mountain's maple stand is unique to the Greenmarket—the only thing missing is a short stack and a plate of Belgian waffles.

RONNYBROOK MILK BAR
THE RICHNESS OF PASTURED DAIRY

Rick and Ronny Osofsky of Ronnybrook Farms went back to the future twenty-odd years ago when they brought back the milk-filled glass bottle to the Union Square Greenmarket. I visited the farm in Ancramdale, New York, in the gorgeous Hudson Valley, where the family has been raising cows since the 1940s. The cows looked happy and well taken care of, and they come running when the brothers appear. Ronnybrook has expanded to farmer's markets and retailers throughout the city and the tristate area, and its milk products now include chocolate milk, yogurt, butter, crème fraîche, and ice cream. Ronnybrook Milk Bar at the Chelsea Market offers one of the best milk shakes in New York City, with the line out the door to prove it (and it's well worth the wait). The spoon and straw stand at attention in the thick, delicious concoction of milk and ice cream, in flavors like apple pie, blackberry, blueberry-pomegranate, and chocolate orange peel. The brothers of Ronnybrook Farms, their reusable glass bottles, and their closed-herd, grass-fed, free-range cows are doing amazing things—no antibiotics or homogenization necessary.

DEEPMOUNTAINMAPLE.COM
UNION SQUARE GREEN MARKET, FRIDAYS AND SATURDAYS ~ 802-525-4162

RONNYBROOKMILKBAR.COM
CHELSEA MARKET, 75 NINTH AVENUE ~ NEW YORK, NY 10011 ~ 212-741-6455

SERENDIPITY 3
A SUGAR TRIP YOU WON'T FORGET

"Serendipity" means "happy surprise," and it's certainly a happy surprise to find such a zany ice cream fantasyland on East Sixtieth Street in New York City. Opened by Stephen Bruce in 1954, the restaurant offers a full menu but is best known for its outrageous ice cream sundaes and its trademark drink, the Frrrozen Hot Chocolate. The restaurant is a mecca for tourists from around the world, who show up with maps in their hands and this confection on their minds. In 2004, Serendipity celebrated its fiftieth anniversary by introducing the $1,000 Golden Opulence Sundae, which was promptly listed in Guinness World Records as the world's most expensive dessert. If you find this a bit too extravagant, not to worry: You can always try the Can't Say No sundae, the Strawberry Fields sundae, the YuDuFundu plate of fruit and fudge, the chocolate blackout cake, or Aunt Buba's Sand Tarts (basically pecan cookies), and that's only the beginning. Serendipity 3 makes children smile and makes adults feel like children. Make a reservation a few weeks in advance to avoid the line, but if you happen to show up serendipitously, don't worry—the wait may be long, but it's worth it, because this ice cream parlor is a legend in its own time.

SERENDIPITY3.COM
225 EAST 60TH STREET ∼ NEW YORK, NY 10022 ∼ 212-838-3531

TREMBLAY APIARIES
NECTAR OF THE GODS

Go to the Union Square Greenmarket on Fridays and Saturdays, find Alan Tremblay and his booth, and learn all there is to know about honey from this life-long beekeeper. In fact, once you see the honey choices on offer and become versed in the details of honey making, you will never again take this nectar for granted. Alan's operation is located in the Finger Lakes region of New York. Like most artisanal craftsmen, Alan cares for the environment, the bees, and the customer, and his goal is to produce the best, most natural products he can. Alan creates many types of honey, each with its own color, flavor, and purpose. Orange Blossom is mild with a hint of citrus, while the Summerflower is suitable for inclusion in herb teas. Fallflower is dark in color, good in coffee, and a great enrichment in baked goods, sauces, and salad dressings. Linden is light in color and known for its sleep-enhancing effects. Goldenrod will complement apple pies, and for something new and delicious, try the Creamed Honey. Alan respects the idea that honey is a precious gift from the bees, meant to be savored, and thanks to Tremblay Apiaries, we can all experience the product at its best.

TREMBLAYAPIARIES.COM
UNION SQUARE GREEN MARKET, FRIDAYS AND SATURDAYS ∼ 607-330-2300

Frrrozen Hot Chocolate

FROM THE KITCHEN OF SERENDIPITY 3

3 OUNCES BEST-QUALITY CHOCOLATE (ANY VARIETY), FINELY CHOPPED

2 TEASPOONS STORE-BOUGHT HOT CHOCOLATE MIX

1½ TABLESPOONS SUGAR

1½ CUPS MILK

3 CUPS ICE

WHIPPED CREAM

CHOCOLATE SHAVINGS

1. In a small heavy saucepan or in the top of a double boiler over simmering water, add the chocolate, stirring occasionally until melted.

2. Add the hot chocolate mix and sugar, stirring constantly until blended.

3. Remove from the heat, then slowly add ½ cup of the milk and stir until smooth. Let cool to room temperature.

4. In a blender, combine the remaining 1 cup milk, the chocolate mixture, and the ice. Blend on high speed until smooth, the consistency of a frozen daiquiri.

5. Pour into a giant goblet and top with whipped cream and chocolate shavings.

Grandma Rose's Honey Cake with Chocolate Glaze

MAKES I (IO-INCH) BUNDT CAKE;
8 TO IO SERVINGS

FEATURING THE HONEY OF TREMBLAY APIARIES

FOR THE CAKE

2½   CUPS ALL-PURPOSE FLOUR

2   TEASPOONS BAKING POWDER

½   TEASPOON BAKING SODA

½   TEASPOON SALT

2   TEASPOONS GROUND CINNAMON

¼   TEASPOON GROUND GINGER

¼   TEASPOON GROUND CLOVES

3   LARGE EGGS

1¼   CUPS SUGAR

1¼   CUPS VEGETABLE OIL

1¼   CUPS PURE HONEY

¾   CUP LUKEWARM BREWED COFFEE (OR INSTANT COFFEE GRANULES DISSOLVED IN WATER)

1½   TEASPOONS PACKED GRATED ORANGE ZEST

FOR THE CHOCOLATE GLAZE

¾   CUP SEMISWEET CHOCOLATE CHIPS

3   TABLESPOONS SALTED BUTTER

I   TABLESPOON LIGHT CORN SYRUP

½   TEASPOON VANILLA EXTRACT

Honey cake is a favorite around Rosh Hashanah as it beckons in sweet things for the New Year. This cake, my grandmother's recipe, is delicious with fresh whipped cream.

MAKE THE CAKE

1. Preheat the oven to 350°F. Generously spray a 10-inch nonstick Bundt pan, including the inner tube, with baking spray.

2. In a large bowl, whisk the flour, baking powder, baking soda, salt, and spices together.

3. In a separate bowl, whisk the eggs, then whisk in the sugar, oil, honey, coffee, and orange zest until well combined. Add to the flour mixture, then stir with the whisk until the batter is smooth.

4. Pour the batter into the prepared pan and shake slightly to level the surface. Bake until springy to the touch and a toothpick inserted in the center of the cake comes out clean, 45 to 50 minutes. Let cool in the pan on a wire rack for 20 minutes.

MAKE THE CHOCOLATE GLAZE

1. In a double boiler over hot, not boiling, water combine the chocolate, butter, and corn syrup. Stir until the chocolate is smooth, then add the vanilla.

2. Spread the warm chocolate over the cake and let it drizzle down the sides.

WAFELS & DINGES

HOT FROM THE IRON

VARIOUS
LOCATIONS, BUT
ALMOST ALWAYS
CARTS IN CENTRAL
PARK AND TRUCKS
AT ASTOR PLACE
866-429-7329

....

WAFELSAND
DINGES.COM

Thomas DeGeest, a Belgian expat, is a self-proclaimed Special Envoy for Wafels for the Belgian Ministry of Culinary Affairs. His task? Improve waffle quality in the U.S. Thomas quit his day job at IBM, fired up the griddles, and began making wafels in 2007. These are not your average, run-of-the-mill waffles. These are Belgian wafels, and they come in either the classic Brussels (soft on the inside and crisp on the outside) or the Liège, an oblong, denser treat cooked with sugar pearls that sweetly pop in your mouth. Dinges are the toppings, including whipped cream, strawberries, *dulce de leche*, bananas, and the Belgians' answer to Nutella, Spekuloos, which is made from finely ground Belgian cookies and tastes of cinnamon, cloves, ginger, and cardamom. It's suitable for licking off a spoon or, better yet, your finger. In its relatively short life, Wafels & Dinges has gone from crowd favorite to Zagat-rated Best Food Truck and back again, and now has nearly forty food trucks and kiosks throughout New York City. It is virtually impossible to pass up the aroma wafting from these trucks when you walk by. So don't.

YOGO NEW YORK'S FINEST YOGURT

FRO-YO WHEREVER YOU NEED IT

At first blush, YoGo appears to be just another ice cream truck. But actually, this is one of the best yogurts I have ever tasted in New York City. The truck is adorable, and the people who serve the yogurt even more so. And unlike other food truck experiences, everything here is spotless, there's no music, and there are no signs with funny pictures—it's just really tasty, smooth yogurt, no gimmicks, with two flavor choices: vanilla and tart. The toppings are surprising, including fresh blackberries, blueberries, strawberries, and raspberries. Mind you, these are the healthy toppings. If you want to sinfully indulge, feel free, with coconut, dark chocolate chips, M&Ms, and rainbow sprinkles among the selections. This kosher-friendly, gluten-free, low-cholesterol yogurt is so good it can stand on its own, but if you want it dipped in chocolate or cherry, go for it. This is a family affair, and Pete, Tony, and Tommy, three cousins, have been doing their yogurt thing for three years and now have eight trucks. Most of the trucks are parked in the Financial District, but the one I go to all the time is usually at Fifth Avenue and Seventeenth Street.

MULTIPLE LOCATIONS
....
YOGONYC.COM

Sweet Sampler: Muffins

TOO OFTEN, NEW YORK DELI MUFFINS CAN BE SIMULTANEOUSLY UNDERFLAVORED AND SUPERSIZED. Worse, they can leave one with that awful feeling of having overindulged on something unworthy. Here are some bakery muffins that won't give you that feeling.

SUNSHINE YOGURT MUFFIN

CLINTON ST. BAKING COMPANY // PG 67
This muffin has a bright, citrusy lemon-orange flavor. It's moist but delicate, with a mild sugar glaze on top.

BLUEBERRY MUFFIN WITH WALNUTS

OLIVE'S // PG 35
The sweetness of the blueberries is balanced by the slightly bitter walnut flavor. This is a mild and moist muffin, with a sugar crumble on top.

BRAN MUFFIN

BLUE SKY BAKERY // PG 157
This muffin is moist and dense; it's also packed with fruit and nuts.

BLUEBERRY MUFFIN

CECI-CELA // PG 66
The most unusual thing about this muffin is its cute, small, cylindrical shape. It is nicely moist with sugar sprinkled on top.

LEMON POPPYSEED MUFFIN

BAKED // PG 148
This muffin achieves that perfect muffin top crunchiness, with a tender and fluffy interior. The lemon flavor is bright and fresh, and poppyseeds abound in every bite.

TORTINO DI CIOCCOLATA

GRANDAISY BAKERY // PG 23
You might call this an Italian-inspired rendition of the muffin, a very luxurious muffin: made with melted semisweet chocolate and no flour, the interior is rich and moist and the top crackly and crunchy.

New York
Sweets

BROOKLYN AND
QUEENS

CUTTING THROUGH THE LAYERS

IN FRENCH, MILLE-FEUILLE MEANS "ONE THOUSAND LEAVES." LUCKILY IT DOESN'T TAKE THIS MANY SHEETS OF PUFF PASTRY TO MAKE THE DESSERT— OFTEN REFERRED TO AS A NAPOLEON IN THE U.S.— WHICH CONSISTS OF THREE THIN LAYERS OF FLAKY PUFF PASTRY SANDWICHING TWO LAYERS OF PASTRY CREAM, WHIPPED CREAM, OR JAM. CONFECTIONERS' SUGAR OR ICING SOMETIMES COATS THE TOP.

ALMONDINE BAKERY

BEAUTY IN EVERY BITE

You don't have to be French to enjoy the art of French pastry. Once you have been to Almondine, you'll know what I mean. The dynamic duo Jacques Torres, of chocolate fame, and Herve Poussot, once the pastry chef at Le Bernadin and Windows on the World, partnered to open Almondine. Renowned for its chocolate, almond, and almond-raspberry croissants, this charming hot spot in the heart of the Dumbo neighborhood of Brooklyn attracts locals and tourists alike. The list of pastries on offer will have you speaking French in no time. The *fraisier* is an almond biscuit layered with fresh strawberries and mousseline crème. It's accompanied on the menu by the Almondine flourless cake, which features chocolate mousse, praline crème, and chocolate *dacquoise*. Mille-feuille, crème brûlée, tarte tatin...see, you're speaking the language already! The cakes are works of art suitable for display in the Louvre, but don't worry if your French isn't what it should be—the staff will smile and explain the ingredients in detail. Your mouth is sure to be watering before you even take a bite. Paris is waiting for you in the heart of Dumbo. *Mais oui!*

Dumbo
85 WATER STREET
BROOKLYN, NY
11201
718-797-5026

Park Slope
442 NINTH STREET
BROOKLYN, NY
11215
718-832-4607

ALMONDINE
BAKERY.COM

AL-SHAM SWEETS & PASTRIES
WHERE THE PISTACHIO REIGNS SUPREME

24-39 STEINWAY
STREET
ASTORIA, NY 11103
718-777-0876

This is the story of two Palestinian-Jordanian brothers, Hassam and Talal, who were brought up in Russia as third-generation bakers. In 2009, Al-Sham opened in Astoria, Queens, and has since become a successful, thriving neighborhood bakery, full of Middle Eastern gastronomic wonders and offering some of the best pastries in the borough. It is a bustling market from morning to night, and the brothers are extremely friendly and eager to explain each pastry. The baklava is notable—you can hear the crunch of the phyllo dough as the flaky texture crumbles with your first bite. I am told this is the sign of a perfect baklava, and perfect it is. The generously apportioned fillings include pistachio (a best-seller), walnut, cinnamon, and chocolate. All are luscious, with just the right balance of honey. You won't soon forget your first mouthful of *kanafeh,* an Arab neon-colored cheese pastry that is served warm and features semolina soaked in sweet syrup, with crushed pistachios. *Kanafeh* is one of the most memorable sweets I have ever tasted, along with *kataifi,* which reminds me of shredded wheat wrapped around crushed nuts and honey—simply sumptuous. Pistachios have become the jewel of the Nile, but even so, there's no shortage of them here. The honey cake is outstanding, and the cookies are even better. I love the sesame circles: crunchy, nutty, and not too sweet. If you aren't familiar with the names, not to worry—just point to something, and there's a good chance you will love it.

You can hear the crunch of the phyllo dough as the flaky texture crumbles with your first bite.

INSPIRED BY ARTOPOLIS

FOR THE SYRUP

2   CUPS SUGAR

2½ TABLESPOONS HONEY

JUICE OF ½ LEMON

2   SMALL STRIPS OF LEMON
     PEEL

3   SMALL CINNAMON STICKS

FOR THE BAKLAVA

1   CUP ALMONDS, CRUSHED
     TO SMALL PIECES

1   CUP WALNUTS, CRUSHED
     TO SMALL PIECES

2   TABLESPOONS SUGAR

2   TEASPOONS GROUND
     CINNAMON

20   SHEETS PHYLLO DOUGH
     (CAN BE PURCHASED
     FROZEN IN ANY GROCERY
     STORE), THAWED
     ACCORDING TO THE
     PACKAGE DIRECTIONS

⅔   CUP UNSALTED BUTTER,
     MELTED

Preheat the oven to 350°F.

MAKE THE SYRUP

Combine the sugar, honey, lemon juice, lemon peel, cinnamon sticks, and 1 cup water in a saucepan and bring to a boil. Lower the heat and simmer for 5 minutes, then remove from the heat, strain, and let cool.

MAKE THE BAKLAVA

1. Combine the almonds, walnuts, sugar, and cinnamon in a bowl.

2. Cut the phyllo sheets to fit in an 8-by-12-inch baking dish. Keep them open flat on the work surface, covered by a damp cotton cloth to keep them from drying out.

3. Brush the bottom of an 8-by-12-inch baking dish with melted butter. Cover immediately with a phyllo sheet.

4. Brush the sheet with butter and continue this process, layering phyllo sheets and buttering them, until you have a neat stack of 10 sheets lining the bottom of the dish.

5. Spread half the nut mixture over the phyllo, patting it down firmly and spreading it evenly.

6. Cover with another 2 sheets of phyllo, buttering each one as you go. Scatter the rest of the nuts evenly over the top and press down gently.

7. Finally, lay down the last 8 sheets of phyllo, one by one, buttering each one as you go and finishing with the last layer buttered.

8. Using a small, sharp knife, cut into 2½-inch diamonds on the diagonal. Sprinkle a few drops of cold water over the top to prevent curling.

9. Bake for 25 to 30 minutes, until light golden on top. Pour half of the syrup all over the baklava. Wait for the baklava to absorb the syrup, then pour on the rest. Let cool completely before serving.

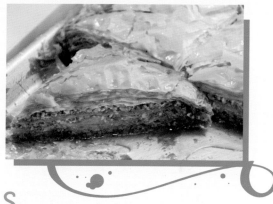

ARTOPOLIS
A GALLERY OF GREEK TREATS

If you haven't been to Greece but would like to see and taste what it is like, then step into Artopolis and feel like you have just landed in Athens. Two years in the making and shipped in its entirety from the shores of Greece to the shores of New York City, Artopolis is an odyssey of confectionery, a cornucopia of pastries, breads, cakes, tarts, pies, and other Mediterranean delights that will take your taste buds from Athens to Astoria. The shop is run by natives of Kefalonia and Ithaca, Greece, and the recipes come from their family, friends, and every corner of their homeland to bring you the best sweets Greece has to offer. The baklava is outstanding, but my favorite is the *galaktoboureko*: layers of light phyllo dough with a Greek cream filling. *Kourabiedes*, or walnut sugar cookies, are used to celebrate births, weddings, and birthdays. *Skaltsoni*, a recipe from Crete, are turnovers made with marmalade, cherries, almonds, nutmeg, and stone-ground whole wheat (and they are vegan!). The pastries, pies, and cookies will leave you with thoughts of a Greek wedding, but don't leave without the celebratory almonds in about ten flavors. Honey, jars of fruit sauces, jams, and jellies also fill the shelves. But just in case your sweet tooth hasn't been challenged, try the vodka-spiked fried dough dipped in honey called *diples*. *Oopah!*

23-18 31ST ST.
ASTORIA, NY
11105
718-728-8484
....
ARTOPOLIS.NET

BAKED

INCREDIBLE SWEET COMBINATIONS

359 VAN BRUNT
STREET
BROOKLYN, NY
11231
718-222-0345
....
BAKEDNYC.COM

Just when you think you have seen it all and tried it all in the world of bakeries, another spectacular place opens up. In this case it is Baked, which opened in the Red Hook neighborhood of Brooklyn in 2005. The owners, Matt Lewis and Renato Poliafito, began their careers in advertising, and over time they realized they shared a passion that developed into Baked. They turned their dream into reality, and they can make your sweet fantasies come true, too. Matt and Renato are hands-on owners who have ensured the highest quality products for the benefit of all their customers by personally eating through thousands of desserts. The menu changes seasonally, but some of the more popular cake flavors include Aunt Sassy's Pistachio Surprise, citrus passionfruit, carrot, and caramel apple. The banana cake contains moist layers of cake with peanut butter filling, covered with chocolate buttercream and topped with chocolate glaze. Need I say more? All of the cakes and cupcakes are to die for, but you can also start your morning with delicious croissants, muffins, cinnamon buns, or granola bars. But how to fill the rest of the day? Take a look at the list of brownies and bars, and then go for it with the Millionaire's Shortbread—a thick shortbread layered with rich salted caramel and topped with dark chocolate ganache. Don't forget the cookies (including my favorite oatmeal cookie ever, which contains coconut, dried cherries, pecans, and white chocolate), biscotti, macaroons, and whoopie pies. And finally, do not pass up Baked's most insane invention yet, the Brookster, which involves a chewy chocolate chip cookie nestled inside a brownie. You will be hooked in Red Hook on Baked.

DON'T MISS:
Millionaire's
Shortbread and
The Brookster

Peanut Butter and Jelly Bars

MAKES 15 LARGE BARS

FROM THE KITCHEN OF BAKED

FOR THE SWEET PASTRY DOUGH

¼ CUP SUGAR

1½ CUPS ALL-PURPOSE FLOUR, PLUS EXTRA FOR DUSTING

¼ TEASPOON SALT

½ CUP (1 STICK) COLD UNSALTED BUTTER, CUT INTO ½-INCH CUBES, PLUS EXTRA FOR GREASING

1 LARGE EGG

MAKE THE SWEET PASTRY DOUGH

1. Butter the sides and bottom of a 9-by-13-inch glass or light-colored metal pan. Line the bottom with a sheet of parchment paper and butter the parchment.

2. Put the sugar, flour, and salt in a food processor and pulse until combined. Add the butter and pulse until sandy (6 to 10 quick pulses).

3. In a small bowl, whisk the egg and pour into the food processor. Pulse just until the dough begins to hold together.

4. Form the dough into a disc, wrap it tightly in plastic, and refrigerate for at least 1 hour or overnight.

5. Lightly dust a work surface with flour. Using a rolling pin, roll the dough into a rectangle slightly larger than 9 by 13 inches (the size of the pan) and about ¼ inch thick. (The dough might be sticky. Make sure to turn it with a bench knife or offset spatula as needed and keep the working surface floured. You can also roll the dough between two layers of parchment paper. This can be somewhat easier and a bit less messy.) Ever so gently, guide the dough into the pan and lightly press it—without pulling—into the bottom; it is not necessary to bring the dough up the side of the pan, but only to completely cover the bottom of the pan. Trim off any excess. Place the pan in the freezer for 30 minutes.

6. Preheat the oven to 375°F.

7. Remove the pan from the freezer, line the crust with aluminum foil, and fill it three-quarters full with pie weights or dried beans. Bake for 15 minutes, then remove the foil and weights and bake for another 10 minutes, or until the crust is lightly browned.

8. Transfer the pan to a wire rack to cool completely.

9. Lower the oven temperature to 325°F.

FOR THE PEANUT BUTTER FILLING

- 1 CUP (2 STICKS) UNSALTED BUTTER, AT ROOM TEMPERATURE
- 2 CUPS SMOOTH PEANUT BUTTER, OR 1 CUP SMOOTH AND 1 CUP CHUNKY
- 1¾ CUPS CONFECTIONERS' SUGAR
- ½ TEASPOON PURE VANILLA EXTRACT

FOR THE CRUMB TOPPING

- ¾ CUP ALL-PURPOSE FLOUR
- ½ TEASPOON BAKING POWDER
- ¼ TEASPOON BAKING SODA
- ¼ TEASPOON SALT
- ¼ TEASPOON GROUND CINNAMON
- ⅓ CUP FIRMLY PACKED DARK BROWN SUGAR
- ⅔ CUP ROLLED OATS
- 6 TABLESPOONS COLD UNSALTED BUTTER, SLICED ½ INCH THICK

TO ASSEMBLE

- 2 HEAPING CUPS GOOD-QUALITY JELLY OR PRESERVES

MAKE THE PEANUT BUTTER FILLING

In the bowl of a stand mixer fitted with the paddle attachment, beat the butter until it is completely smooth. Add the peanut butter and beat until combined. Add the confectioners' sugar and vanilla and beat until smooth. Scrape down the side of the bowl and beat again. Turn the mixture out onto the cooled crust and, using an offset spatula, spread it into an even layer. Chill while you make the crumb topping.

MAKE THE CRUMB TOPPING

In a larger bowl, whisk the flour, baking powder, baking soda, salt, and cinnamon together. Add the brown sugar and use your hands to rub it in until the mixture is uniform in color. Stir in the oats. Transfer to the bowl of a stand mixer fitted with the paddle attachment. Add the butter and beat on low speed until loose crumbs form.

ASSEMBLE THE BARS

Spread the jelly in an even layer over the peanut butter filling. Sprinkle on the crumb topping until the jelly is no longer visible. Bake for 20 to 25 minutes, rotating the pan halfway through, or until the top is brown. Transfer the pan to a wire rack to cool completely, then cut into bars and serve. The bars can be stored in the refrigerator in an airtight container for up to 2 days.

The classic childhood combo, a shortbread crust, and crumble topping. Oh, it's good to be a kid again.

Strawberry PEAR SCONE $3

Norwegian pastry at its best, smack in the middle of Williamsburg.

Chocolate ♥ Roll $3

Raspberry Brownie $4 lg / $1 small

Lemon Bars $1 mini $4 regular

SKOLE ♥ BRØD
Sweet yeast dough / pastry cream + coconut $3

Hazelnut & Nutel Macaro $2

GLUTEN FREE $2.50
Chocolate Espresso Muffin

BAKERI

SWEETS SCANDINAVIAN-STYLE

Bakeri was opened in 2009 by Nina Brondmo, a Norwegian, and Pablo Arganaraz, her Argentinian husband. Frequented by locals, artists, and musicians, this charming little spot, located in the Williamsburg section of Brooklyn, boasts a true New York City café vibe. As one would expect with a Scandinavian-owned establishment, the place is cute and inviting, with its glass-fronted oak cabinets full of fresh pastries and cakes. The staff looks adorably 1950s in blue jumpsuits and wrapped scarves. There are a few tables outside, a long table inside, and an enchanting garden in the back. (Actually, never mind New York City—the garden brings to mind Vermont or Maine.) The quaint bakery is full of recycled furniture. Some of it is from Argentina; the lights over the glass cases were found in Pennsylvania. The high-quality goods are baked and sold on the same day. Nina bakes *skolebrod*, a Norwegian sweet-dough pastry with cream and coconut, that is not to be missed, but if that doesn't do it for you then try a piece of caramelized-pear-and-almond coffee cake, a rosemary-hazelnut chocolate chip cookie, or a strawberry-pear scone. The carrot cake with coconut cream cheese, the apple pie, and the triple chocolate tart are all winners, too, but my favorite is the banana-size biscotto with nuts, dried fruits, and chocolate chips. The jam is homemade, and even the butter is churned on the premises. This is Norwegian pastry at its best, smack in the middle of Williamsburg.

150 WYTHE AVENUE
BROOKLYN, NY 11211
718-388-8037
. . . .
BAKERI
BROOKLYN.COM

FROM THE KITCHEN OF BAKERI

FOR THE DOUGH

4	CUPS ALL-PURPOSE FLOUR
½	CUP SUGAR
½	TEASPOON BAKING POWDER
¼	TEASPOON KOSHER SALT
1	TEASPOON GROUND CARDAMOM
7	TABLESPOONS COLD UNSALTED BUTTER, CUT INTO CUBES
1	CUP PLUS 7 TABLESPOONS MILK
1.75	OUNCES FRESH YEAST

Our *skolebrod* is made with the lightly sweetened and very versatile yeast dough we also use daily for our chocolate rolls, cinnamon buns, and ham and cheese rolls.

MAKE THE DOUGH

1. Sift the flour, sugar, baking powder, salt, and cardamom together into the bowl of a stand mixer fitted with the paddle attachment (you can also mix by hand using a wooden spoon). Add the butter and mix on low speed until no chunks are visible, 5 to 10 minutes.

2. Meanwhile, heat the milk to lukewarm (do not overheat). Add the yeast and let stand for 5 minutes, stirring it to dissolve the yeast.

3. When the butter is incorporated into the flour mixture, gradually add the milk mixture with the mixer still on low speed just until incorporated, making sure not to overmix. Remove the bowl from the mixer stand and scrape down the sides to make sure there are no remaining dry ingredients in the bottom of the bowl. Cover with a kitchen towel and set aside to rise until the dough doubles in volume, about 1 hour.

4. Line a baking sheet with parchment paper.

5. Turn the dough out onto a lightly floured work surface and knead for 1 minute by hand. Using a bench knife, measure out 3-ounce pieces of dough, shape them into balls, and place them 2 inches apart on the prepared baking sheet. Cover with a kitchen towel and set aside to proof until doubled in volume.

FOR THE PASTRY CREAM

4   CUPS WHOLE MILK

2   VANILLA BEANS

10   EGG YOLKS

¼   CUP PLUS 2
     TABLESPOONS
     CORNSTARCH

1   CUP SUGAR

TO ASSEMBLE

1   LARGE EGG, BEATEN
     WITH 1 TABLESPOON
     WATER (FOR BRUSHING)

½   CUP CONFECTIONERS'
     SUGAR, MIXED WITH
     1 TABLESPOON WARM
     WATER (ADD MORE
     WATER IF YOU PREFER A
     THINNER GLAZE)

UNSWEETENED GRATED
     COCONUT FOR
     SPRINKLING

MAKE THE PASTRY CREAM

1. Place the milk in a medium saucepan.

2. Split open the vanilla beans, scrape out the seeds, and put the seeds in the milk. Bring to a simmer, constantly stirring from the bottom so the milk does not burn.

3. In a large bowl, whisk the egg yolks with the cornstarch and sugar.

4. Pour half of the milk mixture into the egg mixture, whisking constantly, and then pour back into the saucepan. Let the milk and egg mixture cook at a simmer until it thickens enough to coat the back of a spoon, at least a few minutes.

ASSEMBLE THE ROLLS

1. Preheat the oven to 350°F.

2. When the rolls are finished proofing, make a well in the center of each and fill with pastry cream.

3. Brush the edges of the dough with the egg wash. Bake on the center rack of the oven for 8 to 10 minutes, rotating the pan once, until golden brown. Let cool for 10 minutes.

4. Meanwhile, make the confectioners' sugar glaze in a small bowl. Brush the glaze on the cooled rolls, then sprinkle with the coconut, using as much as you like. Serve warm or at room temperature. These must be eaten the same day.

BIEN CUIT

BAKING FROM THE HEART

120 SMITH STREET
BROOKLYN, NY
11201
718-852-0200
....
BIENCUIT.COM

Bien Cuit opened in the Boerum Hill section of Brooklyn in 2011, amid rave reviews and accolades, which continue to abound. Master baker Zachary Golper and his wife and business partner, Kate Wheatcroft, are passionate about Bien Cuit, and this passion is evident from the moment you walk through the door. There is a warm welcome awaiting everyone who crosses their threshold to savor their exquisite creations. Commence your day with a breakfast pastry and you are sure to have a spring in your step. Choose a croissant (traditional, chocolate, almond, or, if you simply cannot decide, chocolate-almond) or a light and crumbly Danish (almond-pear boasts rich, satisfying almond cream and vanilla-roasted pears, and the Yeti is filled with mascarpone, Aleppo pepper, and cocoa nibs). No French bakery would be complete without *pain aux raisin;* the version here features brioche dough, rum-poached black currants, and vanilla pastry cream. The tarts are equally unique. Try the lemon-blueberry with basil-infused lemon *cremeux*, blueberries, and meringue, or indulge in the financier, an almond cake with anisette caramel and candied orange. Wash it all down with a cup of White Blossom: white chocolate infused with orange blossom. Clearly, this is no ordinary bakery.

BLUE SKY BAKERY

FEEL-GOOD TREATS FOR ANY DAY

53 FIFTH AVE. #B
BROOKLYN, NY
11217
718-783-4123

The rave reviews for Blue Sky haven't waned at bit since its 2003 opening. The owner, Erik Goetze, has a design background, and it is evident in the decor of this charming little neighborhood bakery, located in the Park Slope section of Brooklyn. The red door frame beckons you in, and the fresh whitewashed walls contrast with the bright yellow woodwork. The feel-good factor is present before you even try the sweets. Muffins are what the spot is best known for, and loyal followers line up daily. The muffins fly off the shelves as fast as they are baked. The many varieties include wild berry, carrot, blueberry, and zucchini-raspberry chocolate chip, but if you need a break from muffins, the large chocolate chunk cookies, coffee cake, or chocolate chip banana bread will serve you well. There are signs in the kitchen that say "No uglies" and "No flatties"—a reminder that Blue Sky takes pride in its presentation by serving only muffins with crisp tops and moist, light centers. Those in a hurry grab their goods and rush off to work, while a lucky few can sit and relax in the café for as long as they wish. In fact, this habit is positively encouraged at Blue Sky—magazines are on display and Wi-Fi is free.

AMPLE HILLS CREAMERY
FLAVORS FOR KIDS OF ALL AGES

It all started a few years ago, when Brian Smith decided to take a break from writing science-fiction movies and turned to making the most delicious, handmade, all-natural ice cream in Brooklyn's Prospect Heights. Ample Hills is a haven for children, with charming wall drawings and a big blackboard displaying the daily flavors—and adults can't resist the fun, either. But the big attraction (besides the ice cream itself) is the bicycle that churns the cream, right in the window. Favorite flavors include Chocolate Milk and Cookies, Toffee Bar Crunch, Vanilla Malted, Cotton Candy, Fuhgettabout the Road, Lemon Sky, Ooey Gooey Butter Cake, and Nanatella. Strictly for adults is Stout 'n' Pretzels: beer poured into chocolate ice cream with milk chocolate pretzels. A favorite that's almost always sold out is Salted Crack Caramel, ice cream filled with milk chocolate Saltines. Have an ice cream float, build your own sundae or milk shake, or enjoy a cone that's been covered in Crack Cookie crumbs, Peppermint Pattie pieces, or oatmeal cookies (all homemade, of course). Ample Hills is an ice cream party morning, noon, and night.

AMPLEHILLS.COM
623 VANDERBILT AVENUE ~ BROOKLYN, NY 11238 ~ 347-240-3926

BROOKLYN FARMACY & SODA FOUNTAIN
NOSTALGIA FROZEN IN TIME

Visiting this place brought back fond memories of my childhood: best friends, egg creams, and a two-cent pretzel at Abe and Shirl's in Forest Hills, Queens. Peter Freeman and Gia Giasullo, the brother-and-sister owners, bring back the float, the milk shake, the malted, the lime ricky, and the famed egg cream in the Carroll Gardens neighborhood of Brooklyn. The duo turned an empty nearly-hundred-year-old pharmacy into an old-fashioned ice cream parlor straight out of the 1950s. The shake flavors vary by season, but if you have the opportunity to get the Cherry Blossom shake—vanilla ice cream and crushed Tillen Farms all-natural maraschino cherries topped with fresh whipped cream—I recommend that you do so. My favorite (other than the egg cream, of course) is the Sundae of Broken Dreams: vanilla ice cream, hot caramel sauce, broken pretzels, and a pile of whipped cream a mile high. Gia and Peter have personality to spare, and the Farmacy is all the more perfect because of their enthusiasm for their shop. I cannot wait to return and work my way through this menu of fond memories.

BROOKLYNFARMACY.BLOGSPOT.COM
513 HENRY STREET ~ BROOKLYN, NY 11231 ~ 718-522-6260

COOLHAUS
ARCHITECTURALLY INSPIRED ICE CREAM

Natasha Case and Freya Estreller started their baking careers making ice cream sandwiches in Freya's mom's kitchen in 2008. They saved up to buy a postal truck, retrofitted it to be an ice cream truck, and set about L.A. selling architecturally inspired ice cream sandwiches. Today they have a fleet of trucks in L.A., New York City, Austin, and Miami, as well as a storefront in Culver City, California. It's thrilling and a bit overwhelming to imagine all the possible combinations of cookie and ice cream for your sandwich. I recommend starting with a chewy brownie cookie with sea salt, but you can't really go wrong with the other cookie selections, including chocolate chip, ginger molasses, oatmeal, peanut butter, red velvet, snickerdoodle, and potato chip and butterscotch. Then select from the fifty-odd flavors of ice cream or sorbet on offer, and you're on your way to one of the best ice cream treats in the city (and maybe even the world). Of course, you can always select an option from the menu, which includes the Frank Behry (sugar cookies with strawberry ice cream) and the Mies Vanilla Rohe (chocolate chip cookies with vanilla ice cream).

EATCOOLHAUS.COM
VARIOUS LOCATIONS IN BROOKLYN AND MANHATTAN
347-252-6660

MAX AND MINA'S ICE CREAM
FLAVORS FOR THE ADVENTUROUS

Naming the store after their grandparents, brothers Bruce and Mark Becker opened Max and Mina's Ice Cream in 1997—and quickly created a sensation in Flushing, Queens. Their grandfather Max was a chemist who loved to make ice cream—the more unusual, the better. The brothers decided to take the tradition further and turn it into a business, and their ice cream's unique ability to challenge everyday flavors has drawn attention here and abroad. If you are looking for vanilla, chocolate, or strawberry ice cream, then the Becker brothers cannot help. But if fuzzy navel or garlic flavors are your desire, then this is the place for you! The eccentric, often outlandish selection of flavors is always changing, and the flavors are tested by friends and family before they go on offer. Some of Bruce and Mark's creations include: potato chip fudge, merlot, corn on the cob, Cajun, lox, sour cream, purple mint chip, beer, horseradish, pizza, and Isaac Mizrahi (yes, you read that correctly—the shop counts the designer among its famous clientele). The ice cream is rich, creamy, silky, and tasty, not to mention kosher, and the place is a hoot.

MAXANDMINASICECREAM.COM
71-26 MAIN STREET ~ FLUSHING, NY 11367 ~ 718-793-8629

Traditional Chocolate Egg Cream

MAKES 1 SERVING

FROM THE KITCHEN OF BROOKLYN FARMACY & SODA FOUNTAIN

⅜ CUP (3 OUNCES) WHOLE MILK

ABOUT ¾ CUP (6 OUNCES) VERY COLD SELTZER

3 TABLESPOONS (1½ OUNCES) CHOCOLATE SYRUP (FOX'S U-BET, IF POSSIBLE)

1 STRAIGHT PRETZEL ROD

1. Pour the milk into a 12-ounce glass and add the seltzer. Using a long spoon, stir vigorously for a few seconds.

2. Gently pour the chocolate syrup into the glass, then stir again, taking care to stir mostly at the bottom of the glass to incorporate the chocolate syrup. The resulting drink should be mostly brown with a frothy white head on top about an inch high.

3. Garnish with the pretzel.

An egg cream is a beverage consisting of chocolate syrup, milk, and seltzer, probably dating from the late nineteenth century, and is especially associated with Brooklyn. The modern versions of the drink contain neither eggs nor cream, although earlier versions did include eggs in the ingredients.

BROOKLYN
FARMACY
BF & SF
FRESH, FRIENDLY, LOCAL
& SODA FOUNTAIN

✳ OH Yes! ✳
STRAWBERRY
SHORTCAKE
SUNDAE ✳

CAKE MAN RAVEN

THE BEST RED VELVET CAKE

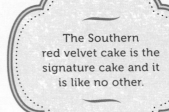

The Southern red velvet cake is the signature cake and it is like no other.

708 FULTON
STREET
BROOKLYN, NY
11217
718-694-2253
....
CAKEMANRAVEN.COM

Allow me to introduce you to Raven Dennis III, better known as Cake Man Raven. Inspired by his grandmother, Cake Man Raven baked his first cake at nine years old and, fortunately, he has never stopped. In 2000, he set up shop in the Fort Greene section of Brooklyn. Just turn onto Fulton Street, close your eyes, and follow your nose to the bakery, where there's likely to be a line out the door. The traditional Southern red velvet cake is Cake Man Raven's signature, and it is like no other. Should you choose either the cake or a cupcake, the experience is the same: Both are light, airy, and melt-in-your-mouth delicious. Of course, one bite is never enough, and when you've had your fill of red velvet cake (if indeed that is possible), feel free to move on to one or all of the following: pineapple cream cheese cake, pineapple coconut cake covered in crisp coconut flakes, sour cream pound cake, lemon cake, and strawberry shortcake. And though most bakeries feature a chocolate cake, this shop's is no ordinary chocolate cake. Raven refers to this as a "Devil Dog snack." It's a moist chocolate sponge cake filled with buttercream and slathered in German chocolate cake frosting (with pecans and coconut). For special occasions, Cake Man Raven will deviate from the standard round or square cake and work with customers to create cake replicas of nearly anything. In the past, he has created a grand piano, the Empire State Building, Columbia University's library, the Brooklyn Bridge, and even London's Big Ben.

Sweets Sampler: Cake

WE MAKE AND EAT CAKE TO CELEBRATE IMPORTANT OCCASIONS, such as birthdays, weddings and showers. The cakes below inspire more frequent cake intake—every day should be a special occasion when they taste as good as these!

SOUTHERN RED VELVET

CAKE MAN RAVEN // **OPPOSITE**
This is a super moist and flavorful cake. The cream cheese frosting is sweet and slightly tangy. You can't beat the visual impact of that gorgeous red color.

RED HOOK RED HOT

BAKED // **PG 148**
A fiesty update on the classic, this towering cake is layered with cinnamon buttercream and decorated with red hots.

FRAISIER

ALMONDINE BAKERY // **PG 143**
This is the French version of strawberry shortcake: a cake layered with sponge cake, mousseline cream and filled with gorgeous strawberries that also line the exterior of the cake for visual perfection.

CHECKER CAKE

BLACK HOUND NEW YORK // **PG 58**
Chocolate and vanilla cake in a checkerboard pattern, with bittersweet chocolate buttercream on the inside and chocolate ganache on the outside. It's dense and moist, but the buttercream is light as air.

MOTT STREET CAKE

LITTLE CUPCAKE BAKESHOP // **PG 83**
Inspired by tiramisu, this white cake is very light and moist. It's infused with coffee syrup and hints of cinnamon and vanilla.

OPERA CAKE

LA BERGAMOTE // **PG 123**
Alternating layers of biscuit, butter cream and chocolate ganache, finished with a chocolate glaze on top, this is a solid version of the French dessert classic. A few bites will have you levitating.

Chocolate Almond Bark

MAKES ABOUT 1¾ POUNDS

INSPIRED BY THE CHOCOLATE ROOM

½ CUP SUGAR

1 TABLESPOON UNSALTED BUTTER

1½ CUPS ROASTED ALMONDS

1 POUND GOOD-QUALITY DARK CHOCOLATE (62 TO 70% CACAO), FINELY CHOPPED

COARSE SEA SALT

1 CUP DRIED CHERRIES (OPTIONAL)

1. Line a baking sheet with aluminum foil.

2. Combine the sugar and 2 tablespoons water in a small saucepan. Stir over medium-low heat until the sugar dissolves.

3. Bring to a boil and cook, occasionally swirling the pan and cleaning the sides of the pan with a wet wooden spoon, until the caramel is dark amber, about 5 minutes.

4. Remove from the heat. Immediately add the butter and whisk until melted. Add the almonds; stir until well coated.

5. Pour onto the prepared baking sheet, spreading the caramel out to separate the nuts. Let cool completely.

6. Break up any large clumps of caramel nuts. Reserve one quarter of the nuts for topping.

7. In a medium heatproof bowl set over a saucepan of simmering water, stir the chocolate until melted.

8. Remove from the heat, add the caramel nuts, and stir quickly to combine.

9. Spread the chocolate-nut mixture on the same baking sheet, keeping the nuts in a single layer.

10. Top with the reserved nuts; sprinkle lightly with salt and cherries, if using. Chill until the chocolate is set, about 3 hours.

11. Break the bark into pieces and store between layers of parchment or waxed paper.

THE CHOCOLATE ROOM

WALL-TO-WALL INDULGENCE

Jon Payson and Naomi Josepher, united by their love of desserts, opened the Chocolate Room in 2008. Go to eat some of the best chocolate desserts in Brooklyn, and stay to enjoy the feel of an old-fashioned ice cream parlor. The chocolate-colored frontage will get your taste buds activated as you step inside to join the rest of the chocoholics who've flocked to this cute café. Gorge on a brownie sundae or try the Chocolate Room pudding, which is nothing like Mama used to make. There is chocolate fondue for two, but if you're flying solo, don't let that hold you back: Try the famous chocolate layer cake, chocolate chip almond cake, or flourless chocolate cake. The handmade ice creams and sorbets with a choice of sauces are not to be missed. The Madagascar vanilla bean ice cream with hot fudge sauce and cocoa nibs, topped with fresh whipped cream, is my idea of heaven, but others may prefer the ice cream to be Belgian chocolate, fresh mint chocolate chip, fresh strawberry, or even chocolate sorbet. Hot peanut butter sauce and hot caramel sauce are always good choices to finish off your ice cream beautifully. The Chocolate Room also offers an assortment of milk shakes. The Black Chocolate Stout float, a beer float made with Brooklyn Brewery Black Chocolate Stout and vanilla ice cream, should float your boat. And while you're there, stock up for the next time you need a treat for the movies. On offer: chocolate caramel popcorn, chocolate almond clusters, dipped chocolate pretzel sticks, and Rocky Road Bars (marshmallows and roasted peanuts covered in dark Belgian chocolate). At the Chocolate Room in Brooklyn, there's always room for chocolate.

Park Slope
86 FIFTH AVENUE
BROOKLYN, NY
11217
718-783-2900
....
Cobble Hill
269 COURT ST.
BROOKLYN, NY
11231
718-246-2600
....
THECHOCOLATE
ROOMBROOKLYN.COM

DOUGH

THE SWEET STUFF OF DREAMS

305 FRANKLIN
AVENUE
BROOKLYN, NY
11205
347-533-7544

Who doesn't love an American success story? Dough, located in the up-and-coming area of Bedford Stuyvesant, in Brooklyn, is just that. Christian Djomatin moved to Brooklyn from Benin, West Africa, and opened Dough in 2010. Christian had first worked in a friend's grocery store, and at some point he decided he would open this absolutely charming and delicious doughnut-making establishment. Tasting is believing, and Dough's rave reviews abound, even for the simple glazed, which has been called a religious experience. The café au lait and lemon-poppy doughnuts are both amazing, and the blood orange doughnut is tangy and delicious. This small corner store is a jewel, with its large windows, distressed wooden floors, and old-timey doughnut cases. You can see the bakers at work as they move to the rhythm of the background music. If you are a traditionalist, you will enjoy the glazed doughnuts; the more curious should venture into the passion fruit doughnut, with its tart-sweet yellow icing. Others flavors include *dulce de leche*, hibiscus, iced chocolate cream, lemon meringue, and many more. Feel the joy involved in consuming these light, puffy, fresh doughnuts. While there are a few stools in the store, you will no doubt walk away with several in a brown bag. No use trying to save them—temptation will win and the bag will be empty by the time you arrive home. Dough is the American dream at its best.

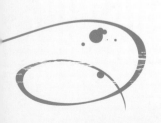

FOUR & TWENTY
BLACKBIRDS

A PIE-LOVER'S OASIS

Sisters Emily and Melissa Elsen hail from Helca, South Dakota, where they learned their pie-baking skills from their grandmother in the family restaurant. Fortunately for East Coasters, the sisters moved to Brooklyn to open Four & Twenty Blackbirds. Although their establishment may be a little hard to find, it's worth it to hone your Sherlock Holmes skills and get yourself there (preferably as many times as possible). The staff is friendly and willing to tell you everything—and quite poetically at that—about what they bake. The menu is seasonal and dependent on locally grown ingredients. The Apple Rose and the Pear Crumble pies are great, but my very favorite is the Salted Caramel Apple pie. It is one of those taste treats that your taste buds remember long after you have eaten it!

439 THIRD AVENUE
BROOKLYN, NY
11215
718-499-2917
....

BIRDSBLACK.COM

Salted Caramel Apple Pie

FROM THE KITCHEN OF FOUR & TWENTY BLACKBIRDS

FOR THE DOUGH

2½ CUPS UNBLEACHED ALL-PURPOSE FLOUR

1 TABLESPOON SUGAR

1 TEASPOON SALT

1 CUP (2 STICKS) COLD UNSALTED BUTTER, CUT INTO ½-INCH PIECES

2 TABLESPOONS CIDER VINEGAR COMBINED WITH 1 CUP WATER AND SOME ICE

FOR THE SALTED CARAMEL

1 CUP SUGAR

½ CUP (1 STICK) UNSALTED BUTTER

½ CUP HEAVY CREAM

1½ TEASPOONS FLAKY SEA SALT, SUCH AS MALDON

MAKE THE DOUGH

1. In a large bowl, whisk the flour, sugar, and salt together, then cut in the butter with a handheld pastry blender, being careful not to overwork during this step. The butter should be in pea-sized chunks, not too big but not completely incorporated.

2. Slowly add 6 to 8 tablespoons of the vinegar–ice water mixture, just until the dough comes together. Gather it into a rough ball with your hands, again being careful not to overwork: Aim to create a marbleized effect, so that the butter is still visible in streaks. Divide into 2 discs, wrap in plastic, and chill in the refrigerator for at least 1 hour.

MAKE THE SALTED CARAMEL

1. In a heavy saucepan, combine the sugar and ¼ cup water and cook over low heat until the sugar is just dissolved. Add the butter and bring to a low boil, stirring occasionally. Continue cooking at a low boil until the mixture turns a deep, golden brown color, almost copper. This process can take a while depending on the heat source, but do keep an eye on it. If the caramel begins to smoke or turn very dark, it's burned, and you'll have to start over.

2. As soon as the mixture has turned a copper color, remove from the heat and immediately add the cream. The mixture will bubble rapidly and steam. Be cautious, as the caramel will be very, very hot.

3. Whisk the mixture together well over low heat and sprinkle in the salt. Set aside.

MAKE THE APPLE FILLING

1. Put the lemon juice in a large mixing bowl. Core, peel, and very thinly slice the apples whole (a mandolin works great for this). Toss the apples in the lemon juice to prevent browning and to add flavor. Add the granulated sugar and toss well. Set aside.

2. In a large measuring cup or small mixing bowl, combine the raw sugar, cinnamon, allspice, nutmeg, bitters, and flour.

3. Drain the excess liquid from the apples. Sprinkle the spice mixture over the apples in the mixing bowl. Use your hands to gently toss the apple slices so they're well coated with the spice mixture.

FOR THE APPLE FILLING

JUICE OF 2 LEMONS

5 TO 6 MEDIUM TO LARGE
   APPLES (A MIXTURE
   OF CRISPIN,
   GRANNY SMITH, AND
   CORTLAND IS NICE)

¼ CUP GRANULATED SUGAR

⅓ CUP RAW SUGAR

¼ TEASPOON GROUND
   CINNAMON

¼ TEASPOON GROUND
   ALLSPICE

⅛ TEASPOON FRESHLY
   GRATED NUTMEG

2 OR 3 DASHES ANGOSTURA
   BITTERS

2 TABLESPOONS ALL-
   PURPOSE FLOUR

TO ASSEMBLE

I LARGE EGG, BEATEN

I TEASPOON FLAKY SEA
   SALT, SUCH AS MALDON

ABOUT I TEASPOON RAW
   SUGAR

ASSEMBLE THE PIE

1. Preheat the oven to 375°F.

2. Unwrap one of the dough discs and roll it out on a lightly floured surface to about ☐ inch thick. Fit it into a 9-inch pie plate.

3. Layer apples in the bottom of the crust so that there are minimal gaps. Pour a generous amount of the caramel, but not all of it, over the layer of apples. Make a second layer of apples, then caramel, then a third layer of apples, then caramel again. Reserve a small portion of caramel to pour over the top crust.

4. Roll out the second dough disc and cut it into ¾-inch strips. Weave the strips over the top of the pie in a lattice design, attaching the ends to the edge of the bottom crust. Flute the edge of the crust. Drizzle the reserved caramel on top. Brush with the egg and lightly sprinkle the top with the sea salt and then the raw sugar.

5. Place the pie on a baking sheet larger than the pie pan (to prevent any caramel that bubbles over from burning on the bottom of your oven) and bake on the bottom rack of the oven for 20 minutes. Lower the oven temperature to 325°F, move the pie and baking sheet to the center rack, and bake for 25 to 35 minutes. Test the apples for doneness with a long toothpick or small knife. They should be just soft. Let cool on a wire rack for at least 1 hour, then slice and enjoy.

This pie will make you swoon, but be careful—you might be tempted to have more than one slice!

LADYBIRD BAKERY

CLASSIC CAKES WITH ALL OF THE TRIMMINGS

1112 EIGHTH AVE.
BROOKLYN, NY
11215
718-499-8108
....
LADYBIRD
BAKERY.COM

There is something about old-fashioned, traditional cakes that just can't be beaten, and one need look no further than Ladybird Bakery in Park Slope Brooklyn for proof. Owner and baker Mary Louise Clemens's signature cake is the Brooklyn Blackout cake, a three-layer dark chocolate cake sandwiched together with chocolate pudding, frosted with fudge, and covered in chocolate cake crumbs. With more than a dozen other cakes to choose from, you might as well start at the top of the list with the Almond Princess, an almond cake layered with raspberry jam, frosted with almond buttercream, and glazed with white chocolate. Strawberry Shortcake, always a popular choice, brings up the bottom of the list; this buttery cake covered in whipped cream and fresh strawberries is a guaranteed crowd pleaser. Don't forget to get your order in at Thanksgiving for Pumpkin Harvest cake or Fall Medley pie. No sooner will Christmas be upon you, so stock up on Yule Log cake and an Eggnog Mousse tart. Ladybird even lets you design your own cake. First choose from a standard cake, such as lemon or red velvet, or a specialty cake, such as orange, marble, or hazelnut genoise. Then choose from more than twenty fillings and at least fifteen frostings. Ladybird, though it opened its doors in 2006, takes me back in time to my childhood, when I would get a special cake for my birthday, with icing, flowers, and my name in script.

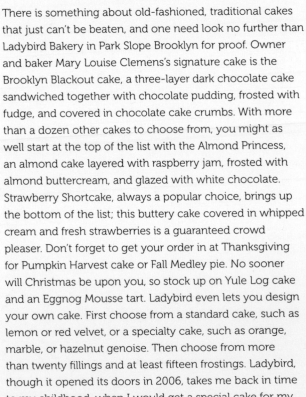

LAS DELICIAS
BUZZ-WORTHY PASTRIES

Deborah Brenner is a new face at the farmer's market these days, and she is getting rave reviews. After twenty-three years in the field of finance, Deborah gave it up to follow her passion for pastries. The day I went to the market looking for some great sweets, someone told me I had to try the rugelach at Las Delicias. Later, I heard the same suggestion for gluten-free pastries. My inner Sherlock Holmes kicked in, and soon I was on the hunt for the booth with the sweet treats and all the buzz. I located Las Delicias and discovered that it was manned by a friendly fellow named Carlos, who possessed a big smile and a repertoire of information. He greeted the many return customers by name as he explained the various pastries on display, which looked delectable and tasted even better. Deborah was born and raised in Buenos Aires and there spent many hours learning to bake with her mother and grandmother. Many of her creations are informed by the Mediterranean, French, and Italian influences in her life. The caramel fleur de sel brownie is one of the best I've tasted: moist, chewy, sweet, and salty, all at the same time. The *medialunas*—the Argentine version of the croissant, only a bit smaller—come in chocolate and almond. The Cannelés de Bordeaux cake, which takes three days to make, has a creamy, custardy inside and is surrounded by a moist but crisp cake outside. There are also muffins and tarts on hand, and it's worth noting that many of the products are gluten-free. Deborah's husband has celiac disease, so she worked on her recipes until the end result was undetectable as missing gluten. And, boy, did she deliver. Everything at Las Delicias is as good as it gets and beyond.

PARK SLOPE
FARMERS MARKET
BROOKLYN, NY
212-417-0044
············
LASDELICIAS
PATISSERIE.COM

Zucchini and Walnut Muffins

FROM THE KITCHEN OF LAS DELICIAS

3 CUPS ALL-PURPOSE FLOUR, PREFERABLY ORGANIC

1½ TEASPOONS BAKING POWDER

¾ TEASPOON BAKING SODA

½ TEASPOON SALT

¾ TEASPOON GROUND CINNAMON

¾ CUP CANOLA OIL

1 CUP GRANULATED SUGAR

2 LARGE EGGS, PREFERABLY FREE RANGE

¼ CUP FRESHLY SQUEEZED ORANGE JUICE

GRATED ZEST OF 1 ORANGE

1 TEASPOON PURE VANILLA EXTRACT

2 TABLESPOONS RUM

13 OUNCES ZUCCHINI (ABOUT 1 LARGE), GRATED AND SQUEEZED DRY IN A SIEVE

¼ CUP GOLDEN RAISINS

⅓ CUP WHOLE WALNUTS, OPTIONAL

2 TABLESPOONS RAW SUGAR

2 TEASPOONS CHOPPED WALNUTS

1. Preheat the oven to 350°F.

2. In a large bowl, combine the flour, baking powder, baking soda, salt, and cinnamon and mix by hand; set aside.

3. In a separate bowl, using an electric mixer, combine the oil, granulated sugar, eggs, orange juice, orange zest, vanilla, and rum. Mix in the zucchini.

4. Add the flour mixture and mix at medium speed. Stir in the raisins and whole walnuts. Spoon the batter into 12 regular-size muffin tins (I use tulip baking cups), filling the cups about two-thirds full.

5. Top with the raw sugar and chopped walnuts.

6. Bake for 20 to 25 minutes, rotating the pan halfway through baking, until the top of a muffin springs back when you touch it or a toothpick inserted in the center of a muffin comes out clean.

VARIATION

You can replace the all-purpose flour with a mixture of all-purpose and whole wheat flour.

These muffins are tasty and good for you, too.

CACAO PRIETO
THE CRAFT OF CHOCOLATE MAKING

Cacao Prieto was founded by Daniel Prieto Preston, an aerospace engineer whose family has been farming organic cacao and sugar cane in the Dominican Republic for more than 100 years. Cacao Prieto creates its products from end to end, from pods to beans to bars. As I was leaving the Red Hook neighborhood of Brooklyn, I slammed on the brakes and stopped to look at this gorgeous building, and I was so glad I did. Its imposing copper machinery does the hard work while its antique wooden cabinets hold perfect displays of bonbons and bottles of liquor. On a tour of the building, the process of making fine chocolate was explained in detail. The factory-shop showcases perfectly handcrafted bonbons in twelve exotic flavors, as well as dark chocolate bars with fruits and nuts, jars of nut and cacao spreads, light and dark rum-and-chocolate confections, and coffee liqueurs. Stopping at Cacao Prieto is a spiritual experience in the art of chocolate making. The factory, which was built from scratch, makes you feel like you have just landed in some magical spot in the Caribbean islands, except it's just a short trip from Manhattan—and definitely worth the ride.

CACAOPRIETO.COM
218 CONOVER STREET ~ BROOKLYN, NY 11231 ~ 347-225-0130

STEVE'S AUTHENTIC KEY LIME PIES
ONE-PIE PERFECTION

There are key lime pies, and then there are Steve's Authentic Key Lime Pies. Steve has been baking his pies for more than thirty years. He started baking them for family and friends as a hobby, then began delivering them to restaurants and stores around New York City. He now has a thriving storefront in the Red Hook section of Brooklyn. The pier where the shop operates along New York Harbor is a bit difficult to find, and it feels like something out of *South Pacific*, but find it you must. The ingredients for Steve's pies have not changed: There's not a mix in sight, and only the purest ingredients are used (including freshly squeezed lime juice from authentic key limes, which are about half the size of regular limes but possess about twice the bite). The lime juice is mixed into custard, then poured into a graham cracker crust. It's evident that Steve's singular focus on key lime pie means that no corners have been cut. Some enchanted evening, take a stroll to the pier, enjoy the best key lime pie you will ever eat, and watch the sun set as you stare across the water at the Statue of Liberty. You can even take a pie or two home with you, since they freeze well and can be shipped all over the United States.

STEVESAUTHENTIC.COM
204 VAN DYKE STREET ~ BROOKLYN, NY 11231 ~ 718-858-5333

LIDDABIT SWEETS
SMALL BATCHES, BIG FLAVORS

Liz Gutman and Jen King became friends while attending the French Culinary Institute, and they founded Liddabit Sweets together with the idea that "candy shouldn't have to be such a guilty pleasure." The dream for yummy, handmade candy bars that use fresh, seasonal ingredients became a reality in 2009 with a booth at the Brooklyn Flea, an outdoor market. Liddabit's candy bars are complex, moist, and full of yummy things like nougat, peanut butter and jam, banana ganache, sugar cookies, roasted peanuts, marshmallows, and pretzels. The caramels are simply mind-blowing, filled as they are with beer and pretzels, figs and ricotta, or the favorite, sea salt. If lollipops are your thing, try one of the company's two flavors, barley-honey or maple-apple. The company also sells a delectable morsel called a Slurtle, which is the beer and pretzel caramel combined with pretzels or potato chips and finished with dark chocolate. Outrageous! Liddabit makes its products—which can be found at retailers throughout the tristate area and at booths at various locations and events—in small batches with tender, loving care.

LIDDABITSWEETS.COM
SOLD AT VARIOUS LOCATIONS

MAST BROTHERS CHOCOLATE
FROM BEAN TO BAR

Rick and Michael Mast have a passion for making the perfect chocolate bar. They buy only the best cocoa beans from Madagascar, Ecuador, Venezuela, and the Dominican Republic. And they care deeply about their craft, down to the colorful, eye-catching wrappers on their many varieties of chocolate. To maintain the integrity of the chocolate, the brothers make it in small batches, following a strict method. The beans are roasted, broken up by hand, winnowed, stone-ground, and left to rest for two to three weeks. This system creates a perfect, glossy, delicious chocolate bar in several flavors. Purists should try the Dominican Republic 70 percent organic dark chocolate (with almonds, sea salt, olive oil, or Serrano peppers). From there, graduate to the Madagascar 72 percent (with hazelnuts or cocoa nibs) or, better still, the Venezuelan 81 percent. Visit the warehouse in Williamsburg, in an old spice factory, watch as the unhusked chocolate nibs are ground, and then gather around for a tasting. These are very special chocolates, and like fine wines are meant to be savored.

MASTBROTHERS.COM
111 NORTH THIRD STREET ～ BROOKLYN, NY 11249 ～ 718-388-2625

Maple-Walnut Popcorn Balls

MAKES 20 POPCORN BALLS

FROM THE KITCHEN OF LIDDABIT SWEETS

10 CUPS POPPED POPCORN
(1 PLAIN MICROWAVE
BAG, OR ½ CUP
KERNELS)

VEGETABLE OIL FOR THE
BOWL, SPATULAS, AND
YOUR HANDS

6 TABLESPOONS UNSALTED
BUTTER

½ CUP GRANULATED SUGAR

½ CUP LIGHT BROWN
SUGAR

¼ CUP LIGHT CORN SYRUP

2 TABLESPOONS MAPLE
SYRUP (GRADE B HAS A
ROBUST, MORE MAPLE-Y
FLAVOR THAN GRADE A)

¾ TEASPOON BAKING SODA

1½ CUPS WALNUTS

1. Spread the popcorn out on a large baking sheet and discard any unpopped kernels. Transfer the popcorn a large oiled bowl. Lightly oil two heatproof spatulas.

2. In a medium-sized, heavy-bottomed saucepan, melt the butter over medium heat. Add the sugars, corn syrup, and maple syrup and insert a candy thermometer. Cook over medium-high heat, stirring occasionally, until the syrup reaches 300°F. The syrup will look thick and bubbly. Add the baking soda and stir well to incorporate; the mixture will increase in volume.

3. Pour the caramel evenly over the popcorn, then sprinkle in the nuts; use the oiled spatulas to toss until the popcorn is evenly coated with the caramel. Let cool for 2 to 3 minutes, just until the caramel has cooled enough to handle but is not brittle. Toss again and shape into 2-inch balls with lightly oiled hands. Set on a wire rack to cool completely.

4. Popcorn balls are best within a few days of making and can keep for up to 1 week in an airtight container.

Should be eaten whole and leave your face sticky.

Honeycomb Candy

FROM THE KITCHEN OF LIDDABIT SWEETS

UNSALTED BUTTER OR COOKING
    SPRAY, FOR THE PAN

CORNSTARCH OR FLOUR,
    FOR THE PAN

3½ CUPS SUGAR

1 CUP LIGHT CORN SYRUP

1 TABLESPOON HONEY

1 TEASPOON BLOOMED
    GELATIN (SEE NOTE)

4½ TEASPOONS BAKING
    SODA, SIFTED

MELTED CHOCOLATE
    (OPTIONAL)

TIPS

Make sure you have everything ready to go before you start. The important parts of the recipe happen one right after the other, so you want to make sure you aren't missing anything essential when you're ready to go.

Let the syrup cool in the pan just enough, but not too much! You want the bubbles to subside but not completely disappear, and it should still look liquidy when you swirl the pan.

Mix carefully, quickly, and very thoroughly: not carefully enough, and you'll splash syrup and burn yourself (or someone else); not quickly enough, and the syrup will cool too much before you pour it out, resulting in flat, dense candy; not thoroughly enough, and you'll end up with slicks of unaerated, tooth-breaking candy on the surface.

1. Generously butter a disposable aluminum foil lasagna pan about 9 by 12 inches and at least 3 inches deep, then sift cornstarch over it, making sure to get into the corners. Place the pan on a large rimmed baking sheet and set both on a heatproof surface, such as a wooden cutting board.

2. In a 4-quart saucepan, combine the sugar, corn syrup, and 1 cup water and stir with a heatproof spatula to combine. Bring to a boil over high heat, uncovered and without stirring, and insert a candy thermometer. Continue to cook over high heat until the mixture reaches 285°F (the soft crack stage), about 15 minutes.

3. Add the honey. Lower the heat to medium-high and continue to cook, uncovered, to 302°F (the hard crack stage), 5 to 7 minutes. The syrup should be significantly thickened and a light golden color.

4. Turn off the heat, but leave the pan on the warm burner. Let the syrup cool until most of the large bubbles have dissipated but the syrup is still thin and liquidy when the pan is swirled, 2 to 3 minutes.

5. Add the bloomed gelatin and stir well to combine; the syrup will bubble and steam. Add the baking soda and stir carefully but vigorously to combine, making sure to scrape the bottom of the pan as you stir. The mixture will lighten significantly in color and foam up. As soon as all the baking soda is incorporated, quickly pour the aerated mixture in an even layer in the prepared pan. Don't panic if one side is thicker than the other, or if the candy overflows the pan slightly (that's what the baking sheet is for); do not touch the candy: It's incredibly hot and dangerous, and because you'll be breaking it into pieces after it cools anyway it doesn't have to be perfectly even in the pan.

6. Let the candy cool without disturbing it (or you'll deflate the bubbles) until it is set and completely cool to the touch, at least 2 hours.

7. Break the candy into pieces with a well-cleaned screwdriver or chisel. Honeycomb candy, stored in a zip-top plastic bag or other airtight container at room temperature, will keep for up to 3 months. Dip each piece in melted chocolate, if desired.

NOTE

Bloomed gelatin is gelatin that has been mixed with water and allowed to absorb the liquid and soften. Make it as follows: In a small bowl, combine 2 teaspoons powdered unflavored gelatin and 1 tablespoon plus 1 teaspoon cold water; stir and let it stand for about 5 minutes. Store any extra in an airtight container in the fridge for up to 1 month for future batches.

Jane Bishop's Naughty Brownies

FEATURING MAST BROTHERS CHOCOLATE

MAKES 12
LARGE BROWNIES

1.75 OUNCES MAST
   BROTHERS CHOCOLATE
   (OR ANY DARK
   CHOCOLATE THAT IS
   AT LEAST 70% CACAO)

½   CUP (1 STICK) UNSALTED
   BUTTER

2   LARGE EGGS, BEATEN

1   CUP SUGAR

⅓   CUP ALL-PURPOSE
   FLOUR

1   TEASPOON BAKING
   POWDER

PINCH OF SALT

1   CUP CHOPPED NUTS
   (OPTIONAL)

1. Preheat the oven to 350°F. Line a 7-by-11-inch baking pan with parchment paper, then butter the parchment.

2. Melt the chocolate and butter together in a large heatproof bowl set over a saucepan of simmering water. Remove the bowl from the heat, beat the chocolate mixture until smooth, then stir in the remaining ingredients.

3. Scrape the batter into the prepared pan. Bake for 30 minutes. Let cool in the pan on a wire rack. Cut into squares and serve.

These dark chocolate dynamos are dense, fudgy, and deliciously "naughty."

Sweets Sampler: Tarts

SLIGHTLY MORE ELEGANT THAN PIE YET A CLOSE RELATION, tarts lay out their interiors for our viewing pleasure. They're slim yet packed with flavor ranging from fruits to custards to chocolate.

PLUM TART

DARJEELING TART

PEAR TART

ONCE UPON A TART // PG 36
This tart features layer upon layer of plums sliced paper thin and a tender, flaky crust that perfectly complements its filling.

BOSIE TEA PARLOR // PG 18
If food is served in heaven, this tart will come out at teatime. The delicate crust is sweet, but crisp. The perfectly flavored interior features a Darjeeling-infused ganache and a Darjeeling-infused chantilly cream, with almond nougatine on top.

CECI-CELA // PG 66
A mild but flavorful pear filling is featured in this tart, with a sturdy, buttery, and crumbly crust. It's rustic looking, but quite polished in flavor.

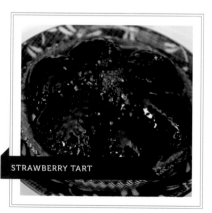

STRAWBERRY TART

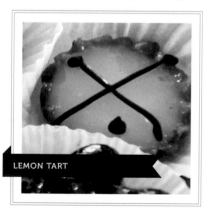

LEMON TART

PINE NUT TARTLET

FRANCOIS PAYARD BAKERY // PG 39
This is a classic French fruit tart, with fresh strawberries nestled on pastry cream that is light as air. The strawberries are perfectly ripe and delicious, with crumbled pistachios on top.

LA BERGAMOTE // PG 125
It's easy to go wrong with a lemon tart, but La Bergamote makes no mistakes with theirs. Super fresh, it has a strong, tart lemon flavor and a wonderfully buttery and crumbly crust.

BIEN CUIT // PG 156
Bien Cuit fills a pâte sucrée shell with pine nuts and a sticky caramel that's infused with thyme—a brilliant pairing that brings out the herbal quality in the nuts.

The whoopie pies are legendary. They come in either pumpkin or chocolate flavors, both varieties with cream cheese filling.

ONE GIRL COOKIES

MADE WITH LOVE

A sign reading, simply, "Cookies" hangs outside One Girl Cookies in the Cobble Hill section of Brooklyn. Inspired by memories of happy family occasions, her grandmother's baking, and the joy of uniting a family over a home-cooked meal, Dawn Casale gathered her old family recipes, realized they could not be beaten, and started the process of opening One Girl Cookies (the store now has a second location, in Brooklyn's Dumbo). At the time, she needed both a roommate and a baker. When David Crofton came to interview for the former, she ended up hiring him as the latter. Years later, now married, the two's happiness is reflected in their delightful bakery. It is like walking into your best friend's kitchen—aqua blue everywhere, with vintage photos of their families surrounded by patterned wallpaper. Dawn has named all of her cookies after friends and family (how sweet is that?), so get ready to sample a Sadie, a Penelope, a Juliette, an Olga, or a Danielle—each delicious in its own way. My favorite is the Lucia, a tribute to her grandmother: a bite-size shortbread, caramel, and chocolate layered bar. The whoopie pies are legendary. They come in either pumpkin or chocolate flavors, both varieties with cream cheese filling. There are seasonal fruit pies year-round and cakes for every occasion on special order. Should you decide to try your hand at baking from the eponymous cookbook, be sure to use an overabundance of the main ingredient: love.

Cobble Hill
68 DEAN STREET
BROOKLYN, NY
11201
212-675-4996

....

Dumbo
33 MAIN STREET
BROOKLYN, NY
11201
347-338-1268

....

ONEGIRL
COOKIES.COM

Old-Fashioned Graham Crackers with Turbinado Sugar

MAKES 24 COOKIES

FROM THE KITCHEN OF ONE GIRL COOKIES

- 4½ CUPS ALL-PURPOSE FLOUR
- ½ CUP WHOLE WHEAT FLOUR
- ½ TEASPOON GROUND CINNAMON
- ½ TEASPOON BAKING SODA
- ½ TEASPOON SALT
- 1 CUP (2 STICKS) UNSALTED BUTTER, SOFTENED
- 1 CUP GRANULATED SUGAR
- ½ CUP PACKED LIGHT BROWN SUGAR
- ¼ CUP TURBINADO SUGAR

1. In a medium bowl, whisk the flours, cinnamon, baking soda, and salt together.

2. In the bowl of an electric mixer fitted with the paddle attachment, beat together the butter, granulated sugar, and brown sugar on medium speed until the mixture is light yellow and fluffy, about 3 minutes.

3. With the mixer on low, add one third of the flour mixture and ¼ cup water. Beat for 30 seconds and scrape down the sides of the bowl. Repeat this step once, then add the remaining third of the flour mixture and mix just to combine. Some of the dry ingredients will not be fully mixed into the dough.

4. Turn the dough out onto a lightly floured work surface and knead by hand for about 10 seconds. Divide the dough in half; cover one half with plastic wrap and set aside.

5. Place a sheet of parchment paper on a work surface and the first half of dough on the parchment paper. Flatten the dough slightly with your hand and then top with a second sheet of parchment.

With a rolling pin, roll the dough out between the two sheets of parchment to about ¼ inch thick. You can use a light dusting of flour if the dough is sticky. Unwrap the other half of the dough and roll it out as you did the first half. Transfer the dough circles to a baking sheet and put in the refrigerator for about 30 minutes. Preheat the oven to 350°F. Line baking sheets with parchment.

6. Remove the dough from the refrigerator and peel off the top sheets of parchment. Using a square cookie cutter, cut out the dough, rerolling the scraps twice. Put the cookies on the prepared baking sheets at least 1 inch apart. Sprinkle each cookie with a pinch of turbinado sugar.

7. Bake one sheet at a time for 10 minutes, then rotate the pan and bake for 10 more minutes, or until the cookies are a dark golden color around the edges. Let the cookies cool for about 10 minutes on the baking sheet, then transfer to a wire rack to cool completely.

PETER PAN DONUT & PASTRY SHOP

WHERE THE WAIT IS WORTH IT

727 MANHATTAN
AVENUE
BROOKLYN, NY
11222
718-389-3676

When Donna and Christos Siafikos took over Peter Pan in 1993, they promptly . . . didn't change a thing. Certainly, the shop must be doing something right, since it has been going strong for more than thirty years here in Greenpoint and there is always a line. Rather than being discouraged by the line, just smile and join it—it moves quickly because most of the folks waiting are regulars, and they're usually conversing about their doughnut choices. The shop feels like a 1950s diner, with shiny metal counters, stools, and a delightful staff consisting of Polish ladies in pink and green uniforms serving each customer swiftly. Both cake and yeast doughnuts are on offer, and to say that they are light, moist, and scrumptious is an understatement. So varied are the flavors that you might as well commit to buying a dozen right off the bat. It's so old school that there's no real menu, per se, but the most popular flavors are the glazed red velvet and the crème chocolate sprinkle, but to me, the jelly doughnut, stuffed to overflowing with strawberry jelly, is the winner. Be sure to include apple crumb with sugar and cinnamon, vanilla cream, coconut cream, and sour cream glazed in your order. Want to know something the staff won't volunteer but you can ask for? A doughnut, cut in half and sandwiched with ice cream. Why not wash it down with an old-fashioned egg cream? Peter Pan is a unique find, and not just for its baked goods but for the whole experience. Every time I leave the shop, I comfort myself in the knowledge that Peter Pan is part of Brooklyn folklore, and it's here to stay.

A BEACHY TREAT

THANKS TO ITS NAME, SALTWATER TAFFY IS A CONFECTION THAT IS ASSOCIATED WITH THE BEACH AND SUMMER. HOW GREAT IS THAT? IT ORIGINATED IN ATLANTIC CITY, NEW JERSEY, AND SUPPOSEDLY GOT THIS NAME AFTER A CANDY STORE ON THE BOARDWALK WAS FLOODED AND THE FRESH BATCH OF TAFFY BECAME SEAWATER-LOGGED. INSTEAD OF THROWING IT OUT, THE OWNER COINED THE NAME— AND A FAVORITE BEACH-COMMUNITY TREAT WAS BORN. SUBSEQUENT BATCHES WERE NOT MADE WITH SEAWATER BUT WITH A BIT OF SALT.

SOLD AT VARIOUS LOCATIONS
347-673-3925
....
SHOP.THE
SALTYROAD.COM

SALTY ROAD TAFFY
OLD-SCHOOL CANDYMAKING

Salty Road Taffy is a Brooklyn-based candy company that's making taffy the old-school way. Marissa Wu, the owner, formerly of Liddabit Sweets, pulls and cuts her small-batch taffy with agility and purpose. The entire process must go very quickly for the integrity of the taffy, so her loyal team watches as the pieces come flying across the table onto a tray, and then they quickly wrap, roll, and twist each piece. Flavors include bergamot, peppermint, salted mango lassi, sour cherry, and vanilla, among others. The taffy is available at retailers throughout the city. Marissa says she believes in "the power of candy" and, since she's just as sweet as her taffy, she will make you a believer, too.

SWEET MELISSA PÂTISSERIE

BROOKLYN'S ORIGINAL DESTINATION BAKERY

Park Slope
175 SEVENTH
AVENUE
BROOKLYN, NY
11215
718-788-2700
. . . .
SWEETMELISSA
PÂTISSERIE.COM

Melissa Murphy started her Brooklyn patisserie in 1998, and it quickly became a destination. In fact, it became so successful that it's practically a part of Brooklyn folklore by now. First-class scones, croissants, muffins, tarts, cakes, pies, and cookies are made with high-quality ingredients and baked fresh daily. The Fallen Chocolate Soufflé Cake, served warm with melted ganache and fresh berries, will leave you licking your lips. The Caramel Apple Bread Pudding consists of brioche soaked in crème brûlée custard, then layered with caramelized apples and topped with rum-raisin sauce. You'll probably need to visit more than once to make sure you try it all, including the butterscotch pudding, the cheesecake, and especially the banana cream pie with caramel cream, layered with bananas and fresh whipped cream. Do not wait for Sunday to try a sundae: I recommend either the Butterscotch Banana with Salted Almonds or the Hot Fudge Peanut Brittle. Melissa and her team will also create a masterpiece for your special occasion (vanilla cake with passion fruit curd sounds particularly delicious). Feel free to return as many times as necessary to taste everything in the place.

Fallen Chocolate Soufflé Cake

MAKES I (IO-INCH) CAKE;
6 TO 8 SERVINGS

FROM THE KITCHEN OF SWEET MELISSA PÂTISSERIE

IO½ OUNCES BEST-QUALITY
SEMISWEET (58% CACAO)
CHOCOLATE

7 TABLESPOONS UNSALTED
BUTTER

I TABLESPOON GRAND
MARNIER

I TEASPOON GRATED
ORANGE ZEST

8 LARGE EGGS, SEPARATED

½ CUP SUGAR

CONFECTIONERS' SUGAR,
FOR SPRINKLING

VANILLA ICE CREAM OR
WARM HOT FUDGE SAUCE
(OPTIONAL)

FRESH BERRIES (OPTIONAL)

This cake is essentially a soufflé batter that is baked until it becomes a cake.
One of the most popular cakes at Sweet Melissa Pâtisserie, it is very rustic,
but looks beautiful when the "fallen" center is filled with fresh berries.

1. Preheat the oven to 350°F. Grease a
   10-inch springform pan with nonstick
   vegetable cooking spray or butter. Line the
   bottom with a parchment paper round.

2. In the top of a double boiler over
   simmering—not boiling—water, melt
   the chocolate with the butter, stirring
   until smooth. Stir in the Grand Marnier
   and zest.

3. In the bowl of a stand mixer fitted with
   the whisk attachment, beat the egg yolks
   with ¼ cup of the sugar until doubled
   in volume. Add the melted chocolate
   mixture and beat until combined. Transfer
   to a large bowl. (Wash the mixer bowl
   and whisk attachment very well, and dry
   thoroughly.)

4. In the clean bowl of the mixer, fitted
   with the clean whisk attachment, make
   a meringue by whipping the egg whites
   until foamy. In a slow, steady stream, add
   the remaining ¼ cup sugar. Beat until the
   whites hold stiff but not dry peaks.

5. Using a rubber spatula, briskly fold one
   third of the meringue into the chocolate
   mixture to lighten the batter. Gently fold
   the remaining meringue into the batter
   until it is just incorporated.

6. Pour the batter into the prepared
   springform pan. Spin the pan to level
   the batter. Bake for 65 minutes, or until
   a wooden skewer inserted into the center
   comes out clean. Let cool on a wire rack.
   The cake will fall as it cools.

7. When the cake is cool, release the
   springform ring and remove it. To release
   the bottom, invert the cake onto a flat plate
   and remove the bottom and the parchment
   round. Turn right side up onto a serving
   plate and dust with confectioners' sugar.

8. Serve with vanilla ice cream or warm hot
   fudge sauce and garnish with fresh berries,
   if you'd like to make the dessert a little fancy.
   The cake keeps, left in the pan and tightly
   wrapped in plastic, at room temperature for
   up to 3 days. For longer storage, refrigerate,
   wrapped in plastic, for up to 1 week.

TROIS POMMES PATISSERIE

A COZY NEIGHBORHOOD SPOT

260 FIFTH AVENUE
BROOKLYN, NY
11215
718-230-3119
....

TROISPOMMES
PATISSERIE.COM

Emily Isaac graduated from the French Culinary Institute in 1997 and, after stints making desserts at some of New York City's finest restaurants, including Union Square Cafe, she opened Trois Pommes in the Park Slope section of Brooklyn in 2007. She has brought to the borough her take on some old favorites, including whoopie pies. Constructed of two circular mounds of soft cake that resemble muffin tops, then filled with French vanilla cream, these treats come in chocolate, red velvet, and pumpkin. Emily also makes her own Twinkies, and her version of the cream-filled oblong cake is dense, moist, and not too sweet—and practically exploding with delicious cream. Although these are two of Trois Pommes's standouts, other delights abound, including scones (chocolate chip, strawberry, currant, pumpkin-maple, walnut, rosemary-Parmesan, and Cheddar biscuit), muffins (blueberry, chocolate chip, pumpkin, corn, and cinnamon sugar), tarts, cakes, cookies, and an otherworldly pecan sticky bun. You can't do better than eating this delicious confection while sipping the shop's Stumptown coffee. The pies are all natural and filled with seasonal fruit, including blueberry, peach, strawberry-rhubarb, and sour cherry (my favorite). Emily also makes ice cream in seasonal flavors that include mint chocolate chip, lavender, Caramel Crunch, strawberry, raspberry, mango, Blueberry Buttermilk, cardamom, and gooseberry, among others. Trois Pommes is a cozy neighborhood stop you shouldn't pass by.

VILLABATE ALBA
A FESTIVAL OF ITALIAN BAKED GOODS

In the small town of Villabate, in northern Sicily, Angelo
Alaimo and his son Emanuele dreamed of opening a bakery
in America. In 1979, they did just that, in the Bensonhurst
neighborhood of Brooklyn. After thirty-three years and
three generations, Villabate Alba is still providing Brooklyn
with top-notch Italian pastries, cookies, cakes, breads, and
Sicilian specialties. The festive interior of the bakery looks
like Easter, Thanksgiving, and Christmas all at the same
time. The cannoli, bursting with cream and chocolate chips,
are famous in these parts, as are the orange-scented ricotta
cheesecake, the lemon drop iced cookies, the spumoni ice
cream cake, and the Black Forest cake filled with cherries.
The shop even offers a pastry that looks like a hamburger
but tastes like a chocolate cake with whipped cream. I
visited near Easter time, and the place was hopping. The
staff seemed to know most of the customers by name, and
I felt like I was in the middle of a big Italian family wedding.
The staff ran around pulling out trays of this and that and
insisting that I "*mangia, mangia, mangia!*"

7001 18TH AVE.
BROOKLYN, NY
11204
718-331-8430
....
VILLABATE.NET

INDEX OF RECIPES

INDEX OF SHOPS

INDEX OF SHOPS BY NEIGHBORHOOD

INDEX OF SHOPS BY NEIGHBORHOOD *(continued)*

About the Author

Susan Pear Meisel grew up in New York, where she started her own catering business. Today she is a photographer whose work is featured in numerous private collections. Her previous books are *Gourmet Shops of New York, Fresh from the Farm, Hamptons Pleasures,* and *Life Behind the Hedges.*